Beyond the Banter

BOB FRASER

EDITED BY VAL FRASER

inhousemedia

Published by inhousemedia

Copyright © Bob Fraser 2016

The right of Bob Fraser to be identified as the Author of the Work has been asserted by him in accordance with the Copyright, Designs and Patents Act 1988.

All rights reserved. No part of this publication may be reproduced, stored in a retrieval system, in any form or by any means whatsoever without the prior written permission of the publishers, nor be otherwise circulated in any form of binding or cover other than that in which it is published and without a similar condition being imposed on the subsequent purchaser. Brief quotations may be embedded in critical articles or reviews.

ISBN 978-0-9935749-2-4

Every reasonable effort has been made to trace copyright holders of material in this book, but if any have been inadvertently overlooked the publishers would be glad to hear from them and insert appropriate acknowledgements in any subsequent printing of this publication.

Book typesetting, editing, design,
production and
photography by Val Fraser.
Except for the photo on page 74
which was taken by Joe Hill.

Introduction

Some years ago now I started writing down my thoughts with the intention of finding my way through the swamps and quick-sands of life as a bloke. I soon realised that it all seemed rather introspective, but there was no context or meeting place to find out what other blokes were thinking. Eventually, I brought together a group of blokes ranging in age from twenties to sixties, and we've been meeting each month. We've had some interesting conversations about life and how, as men of faith, we have reacted to various issues which we encounter in everyday life. In our case, the common thread has been our beliefs. Everything shared is confidential. Creating an atmosphere of trust and friendship is an important ingredient in our times together.

Men love to banter about sport or beer or films but we rarely get beyond the banter. We don't readily reveal what's going on in our lives. The level of our conversation is relatively shallow. Is it any wonder that depression is rife and suicide the number one killer (in the UK) in men under forty? But even though we may retreat into a cave when things go pear-shaped, we do enjoy our sports and can get very excited about our team's performance – even as a spectator. We're competitive and like to succeed. We love being outdoors and enjoy a good laugh - especially at those hilarious failures in manly pursuits.

Many of the thoughts I've had resonate with others. Some hadn't thought about these things before and were accepting life somewhat passively, without questioning. Some were going through a difficult situation but were battling with it on their own. I wasn't the only bloke trying to make sense of it all, so the original rather inward focus developed into a more outward facing view as we were able to support and encourage one another to find hope and purpose in all that we were going through, and also celebrate the good things in our lives. It has been important not to become self obsessed or focused on the negative, but to see progress in our thinking and find a greater degree of wholeness and well being in our lives.

For many years now I've also been having conversations with prisoners; men who have gone off the rails and find themselves shut away from society and denied access to all that we might take for granted. Many of them can identify some reasons why they got caught up in a life of crime. Many make excuses for their behaviour and seek to justify their actions. Some, from a more professional background, may classify themselves differently to hardened criminals. They are ashamed of where they are now given their background and upbringing. But all these men are having to come to terms with what has happened and the consequences of their actions. For some, the experience of prison is enough to make them vow to never return. Others are stuck in a revolving door and find it hard to break entrenched patterns of behaviour or addiction, and, sooner or later, they wind up back inside. Many of them could have been spared from going off the rails if only there had been some accountability, some example to follow, someone to lead the way, or some positive influence in their lives.

Conversations with all these men from widely differing backgrounds and faith viewpoints have given me an insight into how easy it is to get on a downward spiral of thinking and behaviour and end up lost. This applies equally whether we are 'inside' or 'outside'. Not many of us can say we haven't regretted something we did or said. Many of us have made poor choices or had spectacular failures. None of us could claim to be immune or unaffected by life's twists and turns.

Like the rails of a train track, joy and pain run side by side. I've come to believe that every good or bad experience in life can teach us something. We can find hope in the darkest of seasons. We can find restoration after the greatest failure. We can find wholeness beyond every heartache or shame.

So this is a collection of thoughts drawn from my own story and from blokes that I've met along the way. People, books and events have all impacted my thinking and some references to these are included. But it's open-ended and unfinished, just like our lives are at this point. Rather than offer firm conclusions and clear-cut answers, questions are raised which I think are important for blokes to talk about. I don't pretend to have all the answers. I don't put forward any four point plan for being a great bloke. In fact I think it's probably much more helpful to admit that we all have questions which we can't fully answer and that we all get lost sometimes. We all make mistakes and we all lose heart for one reason or another.

Not all wisdom comes from academic study. Some of it comes from the wounds and scars we pick up as we hack our way through the dense forests and tangled undergrowth of our life stories. Having said all that, I don't think it's helpful to stay in hiding, hunkered down and hoping the storm will pass. Sometimes we need to find a way out or a way back home through the storm, and we may need others to offer a helping hand or, at the very least, point us in the right direction.

This book is primarily a resource for men who would identify themselves with the Christian faith and who want to connect with others in a small group setting. Hence I have not referenced any overtly evangelical messages or resources.

Some of us have unspoken and unresolved issues in our lives. Others have been wounded and lost heart. Yet others may have withdrawn from church involvement for a while to find refuge in other things, but the flame of faith may still be flickering. As we bring these sometimes uncomfortable truths about ourselves into the light, we may discover a new desire to live more in harmony with God and with ourselves.

The process of discovering who we are or how we got to this point in our lives may reveal a need for professional counselling to help us untangle our thinking and emotions. Similarly for some, there may be a need to seek medical advice. All that is beyond the scope of this book.

It's not an attempt to get blokes to shape up and do better in their Christian lives or take on more responsibilities at church. Neither is it a prescriptive manual on how life should be. Rather it is designed to facilitate deeper and more honest discussion about how life really is for us as men of faith, and get to a better place on it all.

Of course, the subjects discussed could also raise questions which you weren't even asking at this point. But I'm making the assumption if you're reading this book that you, too, have unanswered questions. Maybe you are already walking on thin ice, noticing the cracks develop with each step you take and hoping to avoid falling through. Or perhaps you are already up to your neck in freezing cold water, trying to figure out what to do next. I hope this book is helpful and that it might encourage you to meet together with other blokes and share your thinking and experience of life.

Bob Fraser

Contents

1 Work: Page 11

2 Stuff: Page 27

3 Community: Page 41

4 Music: Page 51

5 War and Peace: Page 65

6 Adventure: Page 75

7 Influences: Page 89

8 Seasons: Page 105

9 Faith: Page 113

10 Hope: Page 127

Thoughts on Men's Groups: Page 140

1 Work

The abandoned car

My job involved crossing the Pennines. This is a range of mountains and hills often referred to as the back bone of England. Each day I crossed the hills and moors to visit a construction site in Harrogate. One day I drove past a lay-by up on the moors and there was an old Citroen BX parked up. I thought nothing of it until a few days later I went past the same spot and all the tyres on the car were flat, windscreen wipers were missing and the headlights removed. By the next visit the windows were smashed and the doors open. It was no longer secure and was open to the elements.

Over the next few trips I noticed other bits of the car gradually went missing - wing mirrors, bumpers, seats, dash board – and eventually the whole car was overturned on the grass verge. It was just an empty shell. What had once been someone's pride and joy now lay abandoned to its fate, unable to function. It was incapable of righting itself, an ugly sight, reflecting an ugly scavenging process over a relatively short period of time.

A couple of weeks later I went past the lay-by again, wondering what else might have happened to the car. Instead the car had gone completely, removed no doubt to that great scrap yard in the sky.

Maybe the owner had driven it too hard and the engine just siezed up. Maybe the owner just got fed up with the constant failures and disappointments and eventually abandoned the car.

I'll be honest, I know relatively little about car maintenance, but what I do know is that if you don't look after the engine - the heart of the car - eventually it will cease to function. It can look okay on the outside, but it's the condition of the hidden components that determines how long it will keep going.

All this served as a visual reminder for me that when we're struggling or falling apart, when we're angry or frustrated, when we feel a failure or have been let down, when we feel stuck in a lay-by in the middle of nowhere, we can either believe that we're on our way to the scrap yard or we can choose to believe that God has a plan and a purpose for us.

Chasing the wind

It's a shock when your boss calls you into his office and hands you a note terminating your employment. It has happened several times during, what I laughingly refer to, as 'my career'.

The days of a job for life are gone forever. It's a huge disappointment when what seemed like a great opportunity fails to deliver or turns sour. When I first started work, it was still possible to have a job for life. This represented stability, security, and career progression. If you really stuck with it, you could get a gold clock and a good retirement pension. In stark contrast, my career has seen lengthy recessions, several redundancies, and spells of considerable insecurity. Clearly, I am not alone in this experience. Somehow I managed to keep going through it all.

I have often identified myself by my job title. When I lose my job, I also lose my title and with it my identity. But as jobs have come and gone I've realised that this is not an accurate way to define myself.

> *... as jobs have come and gone I've realised that this is not an accurate way to define myself.*

I know unemployment is high at present. But for those still working, a significant proportion of our time is spent at work. There are some benefits – we might learn new skills; learn to collaborate with others; we might make good friends there; we might even enjoy some social element with work colleagues. It can give us a sense of belonging and purpose. Take all that away and we feel lost in no man's land.

There are many other weary travellers out there who feel disconnected from work. I'd like to be able to tell you that I faced all this instability with great fortitude and courage, with belief in myself and with great hope for the future. The reality of most of my work life has been the opposite. I've had to battle against deep feelings of rejection, loss, inadequacy, and under qualification. Sometimes I've struggled to believe that I have achieved anything of any value to date.

I have hated the games people play at work, jockeying for position, the boot licking, the working long hours, the striving for status and recognition, the chasing of salary increase. It feels like I have spent a lifetime trying either to fulfill others expectations of me or frustrated that my own expectations have come to nothing.

It all seems like chasing the wind.

But it's made me aware of how far removed I am from who I really am – from what is written on my heart. The difficulties have galvanized a determination that from now on I will do things which are on my heart. Being who I am meant to be. Fulfilling my destiny. Making a difference. Leaving a mark on this planet to show that I was here. Being an inspiration to others, especially my own family, would be a good place to start.

I'm done with the shallowness of the rat race, of unreliable employers, of unfulfilling work, of constantly developing friendships with work colleagues only to see that shattered further down the road. I will work in order to live not live in order to work.

Not many of us will embark on adventures to far-flung places, achieve positions of high profile or be picked for a prestigious opportunity. It's more likely that our greatest influence and greatest sense of identity will be fairly local, at grass roots level in the ordinariness of life and the sanctuary of family and friendships. It is also likely to involve a complete re-think on everything that we have come to believe so far about who we are.

Danger men at work

Disaster stories about cowboy builders are often on the telly. We may even have suffered at their hands! The client has an expectation about the finished product. There is a correct way to do things. There are regulations, and codes of practice which try to ensure quality and safety. Yet it can still end in disaster.

In my work life I designed buildings in detail and managed the construction process on site. Things went much more smoothly, and there were fewer arguments, when there was good communication and clarity about what was required. When people operated as 'maverick' individuals or tried to cut corners because of time or financial pressures, that's when things went wrong. Sometimes everything got covered up and the faulty workmanship or poor quality materials couldn't be seen. But sooner or later a problem would emerge and part of a building needed to be taken down to reveal the problem. It could be expensive and embarrassing. It often led to a breakdown of trust.

When a problem occurred on a construction project, it didn't help if people withdrew, or became confrontational, or kept banging on about the regulations or procedures. An innovative solution could often be found when the team collaborated and discussed things together rather than argue about who was to blame.

Community is better than individualism. Collaboration is more effective than dogmatic stand-offs.

In construction, apprenticeships and mentoring schemes have always played a vital part. Trainees work alongside those who know the ropes to gain knowledge and experience, and gradually take more responsibility. Without adequate resources a project will either take much longer to finish or will grind to a halt.

Some of this construction project imagery translates well into the spiritual realm. We need to build on the right foundation, and to build well. Building well will often take time. Building well doesn't mean there will be no problems. Community is better than individualism. Collaboration is more effective than dogmatic stand-offs.

My only hesitation in this comparison with construction work is that our spiritual lives are not as specific and targeted as a building project. Not as unforgiving as a construction programme, where there may be penalties for lateness of delivery or poor performance. A local community of faith, if it's working properly, will always include people at different stages of their journey. Some will need help. Others can provide that help. Not everyone in a local community is able to fully engage.

The chief resource of faith communities is the people, the volunteers. While projects can be undertaken with enthusiastic volunteers, such enthusiasm needs the skillful help and direction of others who know what they're doing.

Sadly, I've come across situations where people are made to feel that they are just a resource – valued for what they can do or give as opposed to valued for who they are.

People can also be made to feel guilty about a lack of engagement or even that their engagement is inadequate or not good enough. In yet other situations, very inexperienced people are given too much responsibility with no mentoring or accountability.

A local community of faith, if it's working properly, will always include people at different stages of their journey.

Living with uncertainty

Turbulence in the stock markets, rising interest rates, nervous clients, projects cancelled, news of lay-offs, rumours within the office; and then the all-staff meeting confirming the worst - there will have to be redundancies. I've lived long enough now to recognize it as a familiar pattern. Sleepless nights; panic about providing for your family and keeping up mortgage payments; a sinking feeling in the pit of your stomach. A feeling of failure, even though you put your heart and soul into your job.

It doesn't matter what age you are when redundancy strikes, it still hurts, it still makes you feel angry. You feel powerless and de-valued. There seems an unfairness in it all; an injustice that it was you and not someone else. It takes a massive effort to avoid sinking into depression.

There's a tiredness and listlessness which threatens to engulf you, coming at a time when you need to be proactive and positive and confident in your ability. You feel guilty about having had that holiday, or having bought that new car, or for stretching yourself too far with the mortgage. You feel angry with yourself for not having put a bit aside for a crisis such as this. But it's all too late for such recrimination.

There is the urgent need to find an alternative job, with the prospect of endless hours trawling through web sites, and job advertisements, registering with agencies, updating your CV, filling in meaningless boxes on application forms. (Why do they need you to hand write things in ridiculously small spaces, when you have carefully crafted the story of your working life in your CV?)

You feel obliged to follow up every possible lead; hoping for at least one interview. Having hope is an important factor in the ability to keep going. There is a surge of hope in finding an advertisement for a job which looks tailor-made for you. There's a flatness and despair when you don't get invited for an interview. You have to be braced for hopes to be dashed.

I've been made redundant several times. You would think you would get used to it, but you don't. This time I was 'lucky'. Five out of eleven in my department have gone, but I have survived. There is an incredible relief to have escaped on this occasion mixed with apprehension about whether there will be further cuts, and sadness for those who have had bad news.

> *... having one good friend at work is often a significant reason why people stay, even if they are unhappy with some aspects of their job.*

There is research which suggests that having one good friend at work is often a significant reason why people stay, even if they are unhappy with some aspects of their job. A side effect of redundancy is that long-standing friendships are severed, with hardly time to say goodbye. An eerie silence and seriousness has descended on the office as 'the remnant' wrestle with their own emotions in the aftermath.

Life is full of uncertainty and insecurity. The global events of the last few years which have seen stock markets crashing, share prices plummeting and very nearly the meltdown of the global financial system, have left most of us feeling anxious, yet completely powerless to affect anything.

Younger people struggle to get on the property ladder and can't afford to save for later years. Those in mid-life find their value in the work place diminished. Skill and experience are not always priorities for employers who would rather risk inexperience to stay in business, let alone achieve profit. Those more advanced in years see savings and pensions having less value. What seemed like a tidy sum ten years ago is no longer adequate to provide for a lifestyle you feel you deserve. For some the uncertainties of life are more to do with health issues. Others feel unsafe to go out at night.

Thousands of miles away from these shores, jobs, property and pensions are not the main issue. Millions of people, through no fault of their own are born into poverty and find life a battle for survival as they grapple with disease, mal-nutrition and the effect of greedy dictatorships, bankrupt economies and meaningless conflict. They too must feel completely powerless. The plight of those in impoverished situations can put our concerns and anxieties into perspective, but one way or another we are all grappling with a considerable level of uncertainty in life. We all long for security, but it remains elusive. Maybe we have treated it as a right rather than a privilege.

So what is there that we can count on? What can make the difference when crisis comes to our lives? Some words written around 2000 years ago, when life was probably much more uncertain than now, have been helpful for me. 'When other things have all fallen apart, faith, hope and love remain, but the greatest of these is love.' *

To me, faith is trusting that things will be better than how they seem right now; faith doesn't necessarily mean avoiding pain, but believing that good can come out of the darkest circumstances. For me it also means trusting in a God who loves us and has a plan and a purpose for our lives;

Hope could be refusing to believe the worst, refusing to listen to negativity. It's an attitude and a choice, not a vague optimism. It means believing in yourself even though others may have rejected you.

I think love is definitely the greatest of the three. Knowing others are for you, and having the support of family and friends is vital. We need to know in times of crisis that we are loved and valued whether we have a job or not, whether we feel a success or a failure, whether we can muster the faith and hope or not.

For my colleagues at work who have been laid off, I pray you may not lose heart, but find the strength to believe in yourselves. The horizon may look blank right now, but sometimes a crisis causes us to take stock, change our priorities and set a new course for the future. For those of us who remain I pray for a measure of peace in the turmoil and confusion of current circumstances.

Paraphrased from the first letter to the Corinthians, chapter 13: NIV Bible.

Take it easy

"The busier we are, the more important we seem to ourselves and, we imagine, to others. To be unavailable to our friends and family, to be unable to find time for the sunset (or even to know that the sun has set at all), to whizz through our obligations without time for a single mindful breath, this has become the model of a successful life" (Wayne Muller, Leadership mentor and therapist)

Gavin left a message on my answer machine late one evening. "Sorry I missed your call. I was late for a meeting. Spinning plates at the moment. Dashing from one thing to another. No time to think. I'll get back to you as soon as I can".

I'd been trying to contact him for some time, but that was the last I heard from him for quite a while. When we did get to speak, I could tell something was wrong. Gavin had lost the spark. He wasn't the guy I'd spent so much time with only a few years ago. He seemed to have lost that sense of adventure and passion for life. He seemed so weighed down. He always used to see the funny side of things. He was the one who kept me going when life was tough. He helped me to re-balance the see-saw and keep things level. Now he was the one in need of some balance - too busy to have much time for others and if he did have time he was too tired.

It's not easy to keep the balance in life. It can feel like we're on a treadmill – we're running as fast as we can but getting nowhere. Or maybe we feel like we're on a merry-go-round and long to get off but it just won't slow down enough for us to do that.

Steve Chalke, founder and International director of Oasis Trust says this in his book Managing Your Time, "If you want to be a good husband, wife, parent or friend, you'll have to settle for achieving less career-wise than you might have done otherwise. They're just aren't enough hours in the day to reach our full potential in all directions".

It seems odd that, at a time when there is a lot more choice in just about every area of life, one choice it's difficult to make is to take it easy sometimes. In today's world there are massive pressures to work longer hours for less money, and the constant, nagging threat that if you don't like it, someone else is waiting to take your place. I genuinely feel for those in that situation. Having a job has become oppressive for many. There is also an unspoken pressure to be successful in our work life, in our relationships, in our parenting, even in our leisure pursuits. Even in our faith.

> **There is an unspoken pressure to be successful in our work life, in our relationships, in our parenting, even in our leisure pursuits. Even in our faith.**

Our definition of success seems to have shifted considerably in the space of a generation or two. How can we possibly match up to all that is expected? When did that shift take place to success being all about achievement?

To be honest, I'm not sure it's possible to meet all these expectations. Having managed to shoehorn in a break to our usual routine, many of us are probably familiar with that feeling of wanting it to last longer, and the attendant dread of return to work. These days I'm fortunate that I do have an option to take it easy sometimes, and maintain some sort of balance in my life. It's easier to make that choice.

I heard someone speak recently about whether we are 'Be-ers' or 'Do-ers'. The 'Do-ers' seem to be much happier doing things and find it difficult to do nothing. For them, creating space and time in a busy life isn't a natural choice. It has to be an intentional thing. It requires some discipline, and some acceptance that there will always be a list of things to do. They are probably more comfortable with giving out, but find it hard to sit and receive. In contrast, 'Be-ers' favour time out, a bit of peace and quiet, a pause in life's busyness to reflect. But they may find it hard to self- motivate.

Initially, lack of contact with Gavin made me feel a bit boring and slightly insecure that I wasn't as busy or as motivated as he seemed to be. More recently I have felt quite sad that I was losing a once close friendship. That has now changed to concern that he is struggling, and needs to restore some balance in his life. We need to be authentic to who we are. Balance is always a choice.

beyond the banter

Are we defined by the work we do?

Does our work feel like 'chasing the wind'?

Do we feel tension between doing what's on our hearts and the need to pay the bills?

CHAPTER TWO

2 Stuff

Stuff

Gordon is a good friend. We have spent some fun times together, but he is totally locked into 'stuff'. He's a busy person. He's gadget mad. He considers it a priority to upgrade to the latest versions. He has a good job and can afford to buy these things. I suppose when I was earning well, I was a bit more carefree with my money. I sometimes wonder whether for him it is an addiction. I'm probably about five years behind when it comes to the latest technology.

But as we talked recently it became clear that he would find it very difficult to go back even a couple of years to what then seemed like a 'must-have' piece of equipment. Going backwards seems to him to represent a failure of some sort. His fairly forceful insistence that I should upgrade my stuff is actually quite wounding.

I've always wanted to be a good provider and feel the weight of that responsibility. I hope I never lose that sense. But I sometimes feel self-conscious that my car is nine years old. Why should I? It runs perfectly well. Yet I feel slightly off the pace of other men whom I perceive to be more successful than me. Of course that is an illusion which doesn't matter, but I'm made to feel that it does.

Financial pressures can leave you with feelings of uselessness and under-achievement. The trouble is we've all come to expect a certain standard of living. Yet, it's way more than our parents enjoyed. We expect to start out in life where they ended up after a lifetime of work. It was all made worse with the 'buy now - pay later' idea. When I was a young married man, there was a big shift from saving up until you could afford something, to buying it now on credit. After all, why pay more for it a year down the line if you could get it cheaper now, even allowing for paying some interest.

Was it due to inflation? I'm not exactly sure what was getting inflated other than house prices and the profits made by the lenders. That too has proved to be an illusion – virtual money! Many got caught in the back wash of the financial crisis, and now struggle to pay mortgages or rent, as wages have flat lined for several years. Some might find themselves in negative equity on the property they bought, because the market has crashed and they borrowed as much, if not more, than they could afford. Many are now in debt for one reason or another. Maybe we'll all have to back-track and only buy what we can afford.

> *Let's be comfortable with who we are and be strong enough to avoid the tendency to compare ourselves with others. Let's not overstretch our resources in order to keep up with them.*

But blokes in particular feel an unspoken pressure to compete with one another. It's not just a teenage thing. The pressure of advertising doesn't help. I know one guy who doesn't watch television because he doesn't want to know what the latest 'must have' gadget is. He doesn't want that pressure on top of everything else he has to deal with. Sadly, advertisers find ever more cunning ways of peddling their wares especially through the Internet. It's so annoying when adverts pop up uninvited. It's almost impossible to avoid.

It will take some will power to swim against this tide. We will need to channel some of that drive to be a good provider into holding back on what we want and being happy with what we have. So why don't we rise to this challenge? Let's be comfortable with who we are and be strong enough to avoid the tendency to compare ourselves with others. Let's not overstretch our resources in order to keep up with them.

A man and his map

Men like to think they know the route to somewhere. Even if they don't know, they pretend they do. We are reluctant to take advice on directions – especially from women.

Wherever I go on holiday I feel the need to buy a map. I think it's to do with being secure, getting my bearings, establishing where I am. Perhaps it's an ancient call from the hunter-protector within to ensure that the way ahead avoids points of potential ambush whilst passing through places of peaceful refuge.

> ... a man with a map is an explorer, a pioneer, a master of all his eye can see. Until, of course, it's foggy.

Maps can help you identify remote beaches, rugged coastline, off-shore islands or buried treasure. Maps are really useful for working out the quickest route to anywhere from somewhere. You can trace the meanderings of rivers, streams and footpaths. You can pinpoint post offices and other timeless features. You can find your way when you are lost.

Sat-Nav may get you from A to B, but a man with a map is an explorer, a pioneer, a master of all his eye can see.

Until, of course, it's foggy. Then, it's a different story. There's insecurity, an inability to intuitively know the way; a reluctance to bluff or speculate; a lostness; a longing for home and safety. What we need at that moment is not a map but a compass. To press on in the right direction despite the confusion, avoiding the temptation to turn back and find familiar paths.

It's a relief when the curtain of mist is raised and the sun pierces through. Everything is clearly visible. We know exactly where we are again. No more need to guess or pretend everything's okay. We weren't lost at all!

Fool's wisdom

In the twenty first century we have smart phones, smart cards, smart banking, and smart cars. The word smart has been recycled from describing human intelligence to convey cleverness or efficiency. The world seems full of know-it-alls, but we're made to feel stupid if we don't engage with the 'smart' revolution. As if all previous thinking is nonsense.

There have been similar conflicts in centuries past, as other revolutions took place. Think of the upheaval which must have occurred in the 1800's as the Industrial Revolution gathered pace. Cottage industry became replaced by machines which could do things faster, and with less human effort involved. Traditional skills and crafts were ridiculed by the entrepreneurs of the new smart technologies. But the wisdom of that age ignored issues of health, safety and welfare.

Did that wealth creation benefit everybody? It seems to have made a few rich at the expense of the many. Barring a few philanthropic entrepreneurs, 'smart' ideas seemed to fragment communities.

Two hundred and fifty years later we are in another technology revolution, which is making people insecure, redundant and critical of those who previously seemed to have all the answers. As the world flounders in a financial crisis, many are rightly questioning exactly how smart the new smart economy is.

Burying your head in the sand isn't the best way to deal with new challenges. We need to employ at least some 'smart' thinking in today's culture. But I don't think we need to destroy our entire heritage, or abandon all previous understanding.

As the world flounders in a financial crisis, many are rightly questioning exactly how smart the new smart economy is.

In first century Palestine one of the leaders of that time said: "Don't fool yourself. Don't think that you can be wise merely by being up to date with the times ... The

Master sees through the smoke screens of the know-it-alls." (The Message – Eugene Peterson)

Disconnected

Many things these days seem to reinforce the idea that we don't need face to face contact with real people. I tried recently to set up a meeting at the local branch of my bank. After a fruitless search for a local telephone number, I had to ring a premium rate call centre number and answer endless questions from a virtual person, by either speaking or keying in the information. All that just to get to speak to someone - to make an appointment to speak to someone. No doubt it's all designed to reduce the number of staff and thus save money. I'm surprised they haven't realised how angry it makes people feel.

On the radio they were discussing whether teenagers were losing their social skills because of the increasing use of computer games and social media. It was suggested that youngsters were becoming more secure with talking to a screen and less comfortable talking to a real person. A school teacher reported that her teenage students' social skills were declining despite the increased inter-connectedness that technology has brought. Their ability to directly communicate and connect with one another had showed a marked decrease.

So, paradoxically, in an increasingly inter-connected world there is a growing sense of disconnection, and not just among the young. Many blokes feel this. No matter how many gadgets we have and how sophisticated and powerful they may be, they won't solve the problem of our disconnection.

> *In an increasingly inter-connected world there is a growing sense of disconnection, and not just among the young. Many blokes feel this.*

The good news, which is sometimes difficult to believe, is that God is with us and for us even when we feel totally disconnected. He's there in the midst of our doubts, fears, sorrows, irrational emotions, anger and dysfunctions. Maybe he's just patiently waiting for us to get to the end of ourselves and allow him to restore all that has become broken and disconnected in our lives.

When we disconnect from distractions like Facebook, phones, computers, tablets, and televisions, what's going on in our hearts can more readily surface.

A man and his marbles

When I was a young lad, marbles were one of my favourite 'toys'. Perhaps it was the fascination as to how

"I hate technology. It provides so many different channels of loneliness. Every time you check your email and don't see a new message, you know that, even though people have the ability to contact you at any time of the day from anywhere on the planet, no one is interested in doing so."
Adi Alsaid,
Somewhere Over the Sun

they got all those coloured swirls inside a glass ball. Or the pride at having a whole bag full. They were up there with conkers and Meccano. Marbles were like treasure, turning up in long forgotten hiding places in jars or small boxes. There wasn't the choice there is today. Childhood pleasures were simple and less sophisticated. There was more use of imagination, more playtime, and more fresh air.

Nowadays kid's toys seem unnecessarily realistic, more addictive and more competitive. They also tend to be played in isolation. It's almost as if they are preparing children for an adult world of individual pursuit where only limited contact with others is required.

The rules of marbles involve rolling or throwing your marble to either try and hit a target marble or to hit the other players' marbles. You have to decide if you are playing for 'keepsies' (when players keep the marbles they win in the game) or 'playing fair' (when everyone gets their own marbles back at the end of the game).

A circle is drawn on the ground. Each player puts an agreed number of marbles in it and stands behind a line drawn some distance away. The aim is to hit the marbles out of the circle. Players take turns to roll, throw or flick a marble (called a shooter) into the circle, trying to hit the marbles out of it. If you knock a marble out of the circle, you get to keep it. If the shooter stays in the circle, it stays there and it's the next player's turn. If it comes out you can have another go. Players carry on having turns until all the marbles in the circle have been won. The person with the most marbles wins.

It would be devastating to lose all your marbles! Is this where the expression 'to lose your marbles' came from, describing someone who had lost everything, including their mind?

beyond the banter

Do financial pressures leave us with a feeling of uselessness and under achievement?

Do we feel pressure to have the latest technology?

Do we feel a sense of disconnection with others despite the increasing connectivity which technology brings?

CHAPTER THREE

3 Community

Community spirit

What's going on with the weather? Everything's gone topsy-turvy! Here in the UK, where I live, records are regularly being broken, and it seems that's happening in other parts of the world too.

Remember when a devastating earthquake demolished most buildings in Port Au Prince, the capital of Haiti? The earthquake was followed by flooding and then by a cholera epidemic. I can't imagine what it's like to lose everything. Despite the devastation, aid agencies and local people worked together to re-build the community and restore hope.

A friend from Victoria, Australia wrote to say that despite the terrible impact the flooding has had on people over there, the good news was that the extent of volunteering and people helping one another had surprised the authorities. Human nature was rising up to challenge freak events of nature and to lift the despair of neighbours.

Nothing in this life can be taken for granted. I'm in favour of wholesome things which promote community and bring hope.

I'm greatly encouraged when I learn of friends meeting up to share life's journey, supporting one another, celebrating together and reaching out to help others. Nothing in this life can be taken for granted. I'm in favour of wholesome things which promote community and bring hope.

Our own duck pond

As I write there's flooding in parts of the UK. Some folks are having a truly difficult time. So this story is trivial. We regularly walk around the lanes and bridle paths local to us, but one of the paths has been practically impassable due to flooding. The water is an overflow from the adjacent field, which over recent months has looked more like a large pond, complete with ducks and other wildlife. It was in many ways an idyllic scene. It was like we had our own duck pond.

But today the duck pond had gone. Channels had been cut in the field, and a culvert under the path freed up to enable the water to drain to a nearby stream. It was very effective. In many ways it was a success. The farmer got a significant chunk of his field back; the horses got their bridle-way back and the walkers no longer needed goggles and flippers. But for the ducks this was a much bigger issue. Some of their number had never known anywhere else. This pond was the only home they had known.

My thought is this: Joy and pain run side by side. In reality they are never far apart. But, like a railway, every now and then there is a cross-over and the tracks intersect. We've been fooling ourselves in believing we're entitled to happiness all the time. Promises of a constantly improving lifestyle, and the notion that we are totally in control of our own destiny are unrealistic. And unsustainable. Flooding changes everything.

 *Promises of a constantly improving lifestyle, and the notion that we are totally in control of our own destiny are unrealistic.*

In our sophisticated world we have tried to control and tame life to cushion us from adversity. In the wild there is no such expectation of permanent happiness. The ducks will instinctively have found another pond knowing that idyllic conditions can only ever be temporary. For them flooding is not so much a problem as an opportunity.

So it seems important to me that we should enjoy the happiness we do have. Enjoy time with those we love; make the most of our freedom and our opportunities; make the most of our own duck pond.

Re: cycling

What do a hoodie, a unicycle; a green wig and Independence Day have in common?

With the first brew of the day I opened the kitchen blinds. A 'shoal' of bicycles flashed past. I thought it may be a local cycling club heading off to the hills for the day, but more cyclists followed. An endless variety of people and bikes. Some looked fitter than others, some more purposeful and intense than others. For several minutes I stood mesmerised by the hypnotic effect of turning my head from side to side.

Both brew and breakfast downed I returned to the kitchen window. It was still going. Like a flash flood in a desert. I must have stood for a good half hour, silently observing the convoy and gradually noticing more detail. The cyclists ranged from real enthusiasts accelerating smoothly through the gears of their racing bikes, heads low, chrome work gleaming, Lycra shimmering in the morning sun, through to novices in baggy shorts looking rather wobbly on faded mountain bikes.

Most wore safety helmets, giving the unnerving appearance of their brains being on top of their heads. One man wore a bright green curly wig on top of the helmet, which looked much better. What is it about cyclists, skin-tight Lycra and clashing colours? They can't all be attention seekers.

Another category of cyclist also made a frequent appearance – the novelty act. I noted quite a few tandem riders, a unicyclist and a rather laid back chap risking friction burns in delicate places from the tarmac, who was riding a cross between a Sinclair C5 and a drag car with pedals. One bike had a very tall flagpole attached. Several riders passed by talking on mobile phones. A hoodie rode by on a stereotypical mountain bike that looked too small for him (or possibly her, as I couldn't tell because of the hood!) Some groups wore matching outfits, many riders carried ruck sacks. Some were laughing and talking loudly, others concentrating on not crashing into the rider in front.

My attention was suddenly focused when several riders slowed down and took a detour towards the small coppice across the road. They laid their bikes down and disappeared into the woods for a couple of minutes, then returned to their bikes adjusting amongst other things their Lycra.

> **I missed being part of something worthwhile. I missed the sense of belonging generated by a shared experience.**

I kept returning to the kitchen window to check the procession every ten minutes or so. About sixty were passing the house every minute. The flow reduced to a trickle and eventually petered out after about two hours. My guess was that over 7000 bikes must have been involved. I later discovered that there were in fact 8000. It turns out that this was a charity bike ride from Manchester to Blackpool, a distance of some 50 miles. No mean feat.

Observing the spectacle, in almost reverent awe, I was envious of the camaraderie of those involved. I missed being part of something worthwhile. I missed the sense of belonging generated by a shared experience. I regretted my own lack of involvement. I was conscious that I was an observer rather than a participant. I felt disconnected and desperately unfit!

I was reminded of an important picture someone had shared with me a few years ago. It was of a shipwreck lying sunken in shallow waters, having been battered by strong winds and lashed by huge storms. I was washed up, and lay unconscious on the shore. As I came round, I saw the wreckage of all that I had invested in previously. The ship itself was a write off and was no use. It could take no part in my future journey. But there was stuff still on that ship which could be salvaged which would be useful, and it needed rescuing quickly before the next high tide washed everything away.

So I'm gathering that stuff, choosing to believe that, rather than being stuck in an old story, I am in fact already in a new story; a new adventure; a new leg of the journey. Who knows? The story may even involve a bike. A bike would be well worth salvaging from the wreckage, especially if I want to improve fitness. I may even do a charity bike ride next year! But I certainly won't be wearing Lycra!

beyond the banter

Can you recall a time when something happened which brought your neighbourhood together?

Can you recall a time when something happened which gave you personally, a sense of community or belonging?

If someone is in crisis are you willing to help?

CHAPTER FOUR

4 Music

The bagpipes and the banjo

Live music has always held a fascination for me. One morning I was intrigued by the deep bass sound of a euphonium. I went to investigate. Three cars were parked outside our house and the occupants were already out and warming up hands and instruments.

Standing next to the euphonium player was a man with a banjo, and a few yards away a man arranging his bagpipes. I have always held the greatest of admiration for bagpipe players, not because of the sound they make, but because of their skill in getting all the various bits of the instrument in the right place. It's up there with people who can set up a deck chair at the first attempt. I was keen to hear how such an unusual combination of different instruments would blend together.

It was a bitterly cold morning; one when April forgot it should be spring. Within a few minutes there were cars arriving and parking in every spare bit of road and verge available. Some were more considerate than others. Clearly something was going on in the neighbourhood. Then it clicked. A few weeks ago my neighbour explained that the owner of our local repair garage had a terminal illness.

The garage had been the subject of some local disgruntlement because of the number of cars parked outside the site, and the general run down state of the facilities. I guess it's difficult to make a scrap yard look presentable. Today, however, it seemed that many people had turned out to celebrate this man's life and say farewell in style!

A low loader lorry which normally arrived with a crumpled car on its back was today decked with neatly arranged floral tributes from grieving relatives.

Suddenly from around the corner came the sound of music. The bag piper, in full Scottish national dress, played a haunting tune. The coffin was loaded onto a glass encased carriage pulled by six horses. Each horse looked immaculately groomed and was decked in full regalia of almost royal significance, with red plumes, white socks and shiny black coats. The hearse slowly moved into the main road led by an undertaker on foot.

He was more adequately dressed than the piper, given the weather. A floral tribute inside the carriage read 'Goodbye Grandad'.

Local traffic, which had already been severely impeded by the presence of cars parked everywhere, ground to a complete halt to enable the funeral cortege to move off. Immediately behind the hearse a band, comprising euphonium, clarinet, banjo and trumpet, played a trad jazz version of 'Just a closer walk with thee'. It was a bitter-sweet contrast to the earlier drone of the bag pipes.

I wondered what the connection was for these minstrels, and that song, with the man now lying in a coffin not more than ten feet in front of them. The low loader followed, and then relatives in the more familiar stretch limo funeral cars. And gradually the cars which had been parked slipped quietly into the procession as it made its way to the funeral ceremony at the local church.

Death always puts things in perspective. It always draws out reflection on your own life, even though the focus is supposed to be on someone else.

At times of death, we may be in a crowd, but we each stand alone in silence, with our own thoughts and reflections.

The next day was Good Friday. A time when some remember when another man died. No stately funeral procession for him. No music, poignant or lively. But there was an air of bitter-sweetness to those events too. In the hot dusty climate of Roman occupied Jerusalem, he had unjustly suffered a criminal's death for challenging the ideas and behaviour of prominent people.

A large crowd gathered around, including his mother and brothers. Men and women from all walks of life were there. His short life profoundly affected many. Some were so inspired by his teaching that they left their jobs to follow him wherever he travelled. They listened to his teaching and believed his promises. Heard his talk of freedom and justice. Witnessed the blind see and the lame walk. But their dream was now shattered. They couldn't believe it. This wasn't how it was all supposed to end. They lurked on the perimeter of the crowd, hiding their faces, fearful of reprisals or further unjust trials, deeply aware that they might have made the biggest mistake of their lives.

He had said things no one had dared to think before, he had made them feel important and valued, burning away years of tradition, oppression and confusion. It made so much more sense than all they had ever known. He had given so much hope in a hopeless world. The local mafia were there too, smugly congratulating one another that they had rid their community of someone who challenged their control and hypocrisy, yet strangely jealous of his popularity and influence amongst ordinary people.

At times of death, we may be in a crowd, but we each stand alone in silence with our own thoughts and reflections. The weirdest of memories and emotions can surface. Life is short; death always comes at an inappropriate time; always catches us on the wrong foot. We're never fully prepared. But, in the aftermath there comes a time when a life is celebrated rather than a loss mourned. When joy replaces sadness; when brokenness is restored; when water is changed to wine.

The bagpipes and the banjo, were a reminder that life can be both bitter and sweet. One day it will all make sense.

Jam night

It was like stepping into another world. An old friend had invited me to his local for Jam Night. The only available seats were right below a flat screen television on the wall. My friend pointed out a tall thin woman across the room as the manager of the pub, and said she could look after herself and wouldn't stand for any nonsense. He asked if she would turn the TV volume down so we could hear ourselves talk. Her look said it all. Our request was ignored.

Seventy per cent of the punters were men, twenty five per cent women. The remainder could have been either. Most of the men looked over forty, short in stature though large in girth. I noticed quite a few tattoos, mainly on women. My observations were brief as I feared making eye contact might trigger a fight.

The pub was old and traditional, but decked out in readiness for a Halloween event in a few days' time. There were skulls, skeletons, witches and other paraphernalia dangling everywhere. The ubiquitous big-screen TV and pool table occupied another room to the rear.

On one side of the entrance a buffet was laid out for someone's fiftieth birthday party. On the other side was the stage with an assortment of microphone stands, amplifiers and guitars. The number of amps and guitars increased as musicians arrived.

At around 9pm the 'band' began to gather on stage with much banter, laughter and checking of tunings and volumes, and with guitar licks piercing through the increasing cacophony of sound. The opening R and B number started off with three guitarists, a bass player, and a lead singer, who were greatly enhanced a few minutes later by a saxophone player and the drummer (always the last to be ready). The song finished about ten minutes later to a surprisingly small ripple of applause, mainly from our table.

As they worked through the set, the sound got tighter and louder, and two different blues harmonica players augmented the sound on various songs. Somewhat randomly, the lead singer nodded in the direction of one musician or another signalling that it was their turn to play a lead instrumental. Each song seemed to have at least half a dozen instrumental breaks.

Jam night is not supposed to be a polished performance of carefully crafted songs and arrangements. It's more about the fun of playing together. Occasional gaffs are permitted; two lead guitarists can play at once; improvisation is welcomed. No one is bothered about the sound volume.

After about forty minutes the line-up changed significantly. The new guitarist, Chris, was a young lad in his early twenties. How would he blend with the ageing rockers?

> *Watching live musicians play is inspiring. Music is a great leveller. It doesn't matter what your background is.*

As the lead singer sang with passion 'Lord have Mercy' Chris played his Fender Stratocaster, oozing confidence. After a few songs he swapped to a Fender Telecaster, and he just played from his heart. Hardly needing to look at the fret board, his fingers were a blur of action, with echoes of Hendrix and early Clapton.

He seemed to enjoy every moment, sometimes surprised at his own skill at improvisation, frequently smiling and acknowledging great playing by the others. His dad stood at the bar, clearly proud of his lad's natural skill as a musician. Chris played blues and rock and roll guitar on songs written well before he was born, effortlessly bringing freshness to old classics such as The Stones 'Route 66' and Clapton's 'Crossroads.' It was a great night and the ringing in my ears only began to subside by the following lunch time.

Watching live musicians play is inspiring. Music is a great leveller. It doesn't matter what your background is. Age is unimportant. Songs from fifty years ago can sound even better now. Friendships are forged through music. Some musicians are genuinely gifted. Music should be fun but it takes much secret practice to be able to perform freely from the heart.

Weekend warriors

Music Live used to be held annually at the National Exhibition Centre in Birmingham. It was a showcase for all the big manufacturers and retailers of music and recording gear to display their latest products.

Our trip had become an event of pilgrimage status. The challenge was to get the minibus parked as near to the exhibition hall as possible. Will the parking steward fall, yet again, for Pete's line that we have a person with limited mobility on board?

I slide down in my seat to avoid the embarrassment of possibly being asked to line up outside the bus to determine who the disabled person is. Miraculously, the steward accepted the story. To be fair, this particular year, one among us had fallen off a ladder and shattered his kneecap, necessitating the use of a crutch.

The pilgrim band this year comprised a mixed bag of musicians, wannabe musicians, aging musicians and sons of ageing musicians. For most of us our involvement in music is confined to spare time and weekends.

Music Live was a chance to see top musicians and singers strut their stuff. Or rather someone else's stuff! In fact I noticed that many of the performers completely forgot that they were primarily there to boost the interest in a particular product. They did, however, remember to mention their latest CD. And they just happened to have a few copies handy. I know ageing musicians are prone to memory loss but these guys were pretty selective in what they chose to remember.

A non-musician would describe the main hall as noisy. But teens and musicians would find it quite normal. The cacophony of sound gets louder as the day progresses, with each stall trying to out-do the next one in trying to attract a crowd. It reminds me of the tactics used by street performers at the Edinburgh festival. It's all good fun, with a challenge to see who can get the best deal off the already discounted prices.

The trip for me promised more hope for re-connecting with friends I don't see that often, than it did of getting a bargain. As I chatted with my friends during the day I discovered that most were far more knowledgeable than I was about guitars. I would be unable to have more than a two sentence conversation about the pros and cons of a Fender Stratocaster or a Gibson SG. I am more fascinated by song writing, recording and vocal production.

But I also discovered that one was still grieving and unable to come to terms with the loss of a close friend who died suddenly earlier this year. A mutual friend of another is running on empty. His life is on hold as he grapples with problems in his marriage. And I really missed the connection which goes deeper than male banter, and the friendship which goes further than just shared experience.

I think it was on my tenth circuit of the hall that I noticed a leaflet on a stall run by the Music Industries Association entitled 'Weekend Warriors'. It described their activities as 'a programme that gives older, lapsed musicians a unique opportunity to re-join a band and re-live their musical youth'. It had a sub-title on the leaflet 'Get back to where you once belonged'.

How poignant those words were at that moment, almost like a signpost to re-connect with a lost something-or-other, a clue to where the answer might lie. Sometimes we just need to get back to where we once belonged. To rediscover that warrior within us who has been wounded by the arrows of life, forced to seek refuge in safe and familiar places, but seldom finding the courage to come out and face the enemy again, for fear of being knocked out permanently.

> **Becoming a full time warrior is a process. It may require time to examine past wounds, courage to face hurting places of the heart and strength to salvage what's needed for the road ahead.**

Being a 'Weekend Warrior' is a start for some, thus enabling a re-connection with the fun of years gone by. A chance to re-awaken the creativity which sleeps in the distant reaches of our mind or in the pages a photo album. Becoming a full time warrior is a process. It may require time to examine past wounds, courage to face hurting places of the heart and strength to salvage what's needed for the road ahead.

I realised in hindsight, that if it's my intention to carry on playing music, buying wall hangers for my guitars was a poor choice!

What happened next?

The very first band I played in re-formed for a one off gig. We met each month to practice with the aim of re-creating the sound of the Sixties. We returned to the place where we were the youth club house band. The gig was a sell-out!

It was just great to meet again some of the 'young people' who used to get high on pop and crisps and a few songs from our band. Some had travelled huge distances to be there that night, including a couple who flew in from Spain and a guy from Germany.

The late sixties were our mid to late teenage years. Many of us found a faith which shaped the future direction of our lives. Of the five of us in the band, I was the only one to have continued playing in a band since those days. But we managed to re-construct four original songs after listening to a rough tape recording made of a concert we did at The Catacombs coffee bar in Manchester in 1968 – the pinnacle of our musical achievement at that time. We bolted on two Beatles songs and we had our sixties set. The audience response was astonishing. A sincere, enthusiastic, explosive standing ovation lasting several minutes. We were blown away.

When I joined the youth club in 1966 around eighty youngsters met each week. Three years later most had left to pursue careers and further education. Have you seen the TV game show A Question of Sport? Where they freeze a sporting video and ask the panel what happened next? I've often wondered what happened next in the lives of these old friends.

In reality the cameras are still rolling. All our life stories are still unfolding. The video didn't freeze at any point, and we are not defined by any event which occurred in the past – for good or ill. The past has gone and it's not good to dwell on it unnecessarily. Neither is it wise to worry too much about our future, and put off things we could do now until a time when life is less pressured, or a particular situation is resolved.

So, rather than looking back on failure, or fearing the future, I want to enjoy friendship, music and laughter. To embrace faith, hope and love.

beyond the banter

How significant is music in your life?

Is music a great leveller for blokes?

Are you waiting for a time when life is less pressured to do the things you love?

CHAPTER FIVE

Photo: Great Uncle Clement Eastham

5 War and Peace

The epic struggle

Have you watched films or documentaries about war? Then you'll understand how repeated bombardment wears the opposition down, leading to retreat or even surrender. Transfer that picture to the story of your life. Ever had that feeling that you were under attack? Just when you thought that it was safe to come out of hiding, another wave of Jet Fighters drops its load. There was no air raid siren and we didn't see it coming. Everything stops. The familiar and normal has gone.

When I read about the devastation caused by war and conflict in different parts of the world, when buildings and communities are devastated, mains services cut off,

I'm amazed at how people somehow manage to carry on. Perhaps it's in our nature to battle on but there may come a point when the situation seems hopeless and we need to wave a white flag. There's no shame in that. In fact it can be the starting point of hope for the future.

> *I'd be surprised if there are many blokes who can honestly say they have never ever lost heart.*

It helped me to discover that my story is very important, that my being on this planet has meaning and purpose. But more than that, my story is set within a much larger story.

All men struggle at one time or another with different aspects of their life. This can be due to some personal failing or weakness (something we did) or the impact of circumstances or other people on our lives (something that happened to us). I don't think it really matters how we got to the point of giving up and losing heart. Yes it might help to ask how and why, and re-trace our steps to figure out what went wrong. But the more important question is how do we get going again?

I'd be surprised if there are many blokes who can honestly say they have never ever lost heart, or become disillusioned, or felt a sense of failure. Many of us have already been there and got the T-shirt. Yet, we may find ourselves there again at some later date, perhaps for a different reason. It's almost as if we were in some sort of epic battle for our hearts.

John Eldredge in his book 'Epic' says "Sure, some good things happen, sometimes beautiful things. But tragic things happen too. What does it mean? We find ourselves in the middle of a story that is sometimes wonderful, sometimes awful, usually a confusing mixture of both, and we haven't a clue how to make sense of it all. No wonder we keep losing heart".

A fragile peace

The news is dominated yet again by events in the Middle East. How must it feel to live in a place like that? How does an ordinary man live a peaceful, meaningful life? How does he earn a living, care for a family and bring security and protection to those he loves? How does he manage to hold on to his beliefs and values?

How must it feel to have your homeland occupied by the enemy? To be dispossessed of your land? To have your home bombarded and reduced to a pile of rubble? How must it feel to lose relatives, friends, possessions and dignity? To be surrounded by devastation, chaos and uncertainty. Knowing no security. Not knowing where the next meal may come from, or whether you will even have a table to sit at? How would we cope with no electricity, no running water, living the life of a refugee in a climate of fear? What must it be like to be frightened by the retaliation of extremists, and equally fearful of your own reactions and emotions which may boil over in desperation demanding justice and revenge?

From time to time a cease fire is declared, providing desperate civilians a much needed opportunity to assess the damage, look after the wounded, re-group, and somehow go on with their lives. It's a fragile peace and experience suggests it will not last, that war will resume, that there will be yet more suffering.

Choices are limited in a situation where most of what is happening is outside your control. The only choices available are probably equally daunting; to stay in enemy occupied territory, remain a victim of war, existing and surviving rather than living, but at least being close to roots and family and all that is familiar. The alternative is to leave all that behind and head for somewhere, anywhere, in the hope of a better life.

Sometimes, my heart has felt like that enemy occupied land; battle weary, battered and bruised after yet another enemy onslaught. Every now and then there is a temporary cease-fire, giving chance to re-group, offering new hope and encouragement to keep going.

Within twenty four hours of this another bombardment comes. It threatens to destroy much of what I had managed to salvage from previous wreckage. The enemy knows how to target with precision any weakness in our defences. His aim is to immobilise, silence, and distract. He wants to create dis-unity, spread lies and confusion. To cut off supplies and break the battle line.

In these circumstances we have two choices. Neither choice comes without risk. Neither is right or wrong. We can stay in enemy occupied territory in a survival existence, and remain victims of war, hunkering down until the next cease-fire. Or, we can gather all those we love and anything we can salvage, and start out on a new adventure with hope and optimism, clinging to the promise that even though the path is unfamiliar and the destination unclear, the best is yet to come.

An Englishman's heart is his castle

I've been thinking about castles and fortresses. Those massive walls are steeped in a history which is filled with tales of warfare, romance and chivalry. Places where ancient myths abound of pampered princesses and heroic knights.

There's a strange fascination with castles. For boys it's all about swords and shields, battles and bows and arrows. For girls it's about long hair and floaty dresses. It used to be that the girl in the floaty dress would get rescued by the bloke riding the white horse. Nowadays the girl has to be a strong role model, probably pushing the bearded bumbling bloke in the chain mail vest into a horse trough so that she can get the job done!

In the ninth and tenth centuries in Europe and the Middle East certain nobles had the idea of developing simple fortified keeps into more significant structures. Castles were the result, designed to offer not only a secure refuge from enemies but also a base from which raids could be launched. So they were both defensive and offensive. They became seats of power and control, centres of local administration and finance. They were not always occupied by benevolent rulers. Often angry tyrants were eager to oppress the local villagers and maintain control, whilst endeavouring to acquire land belonging to others by force.

Of course, a castle built seven hundred years ago would offer little protection from today's array of weaponry. But their walls would be thick enough to incorporate secret passages and staircases, and slit windows for archers to rain down arrows on the approaching danger. Some had moats and drawbridges with heavy portcullises at the only official point of entry. The fortresses of old were built on high ground, offered protection from a sustained enemy assault and a haven for that all important respite following a battle.

Here in the UK, our Kings and Queens have always lived in castles and palaces, which have become symbols of luxury and ceremony. As a result of the popularity of books and films like the Harry Potter series, or games such as Dungeons and Dragons, castles have also become associated with fantasy. Myth and legend intertwine with themes of heroism and rescue from evil forces. It seems there is still a consciousness of good needing to triumph over bad.

But the world we live in today is often a cruel place filled with conflicts and heartaches. Many are on the move seeking refuge in less stressful places where they can get on with their lives without fear of death or violent repression. Places where they can be free to express an opinion, or hold a belief.

On a lesser scale, we've probably all experienced a longing sometimes for a place of refuge. Holiday escapes can offer some respite. A few beers might wash away the stress of a difficult week. But some of us have realised that our hearts are vulnerable places, and we seek to surround them with thick walls in order to protect them. Yet, sometimes, the slings and arrows of enemy activity can still breach our flimsy defences and find their mark.

> *. . . occasionally we just want to pull up the drawbridge and retreat to an inner sanctum where we feel relatively safe*

Too many times old wounds affect our willingness to become a target once more. Is it any wonder that occasionally we just want to pull up the drawbridge and retreat to an inner sanctum where we feel relatively safe? A sanctuary where we don't have to deal with things and people for a while? Meanwhile, those who can afford it will surround their hearts with luxury, as if that might offer some protection. Still others will find refuge for their hearts in ceremony, giving the impression of order and dignity. Yet others will hide in some kind of fantasy world to avoid the reality and harshness of real life.

I chatted with someone recently who felt that he was stuck in a defensive mode rather than going on the offensive. By offensive he didn't mean becoming aggressive. He just wanted to be more determined to fight for the hearts and minds of those in his world who were struggling and be more outward focused towards others. He felt his main tendency when the going got tough was to hunker down and shelter from the storm, and it took a massive effort to be open about how life was for him and be compassionate towards others. Some of it was down to fear of being hurt again.

So, is there some way we can be more real with others and own up to the way things are? Can our hearts and minds be released from that sense of captivity or that siege mentality, and become less defensive? Is there some strategy we can employ, some armour we can put on, which will 'guard our heart', that last bastion within us protecting our innermost thoughts, beliefs and emotions? Can we muster the courage to come out of hiding rather than hide like a scared fox? Can we avoid being wounded? Maybe not, but sometimes we just have to take that risk.

beyond the banter

How must it feel to have your homeland occupied by the enemy?

To have your home bombarded and reduced to a pile of rubble?

How must it feel to lose relatives, friends, possessions and dignity?

CHAPTER SIX

PHOTO: COURTESY OF JOE HILL

6 Adventure

Men wanted for hazardous journey

When was the last time you were invited on an adventure?

I was reminded recently about an advertisement that supposedly appeared in a newspaper in December 1913.

The story goes that five thousand men applied for twenty six places to join Ernest Shackleton on another of his polar expeditions. There is some doubt about the authenticity of this advertisement. But even if it was an ironic spoof, it still makes the point. Men love adventure. Men thrive on a challenge.

The Endurance set sail on August 8th 1914, five days after war had been declared on Germany, with the blessing of the First Lord of the Admiralty, Winston Churchill.

Not long after this another challenge was issued to men in the UK. A poster of Lord Kitchener's recruiting sergeant, with his staring eyes and pointing finger, bore the caption 'Your country needs you'. It captured the imagination of many who were eager to serve King and country.

The idea of a big adventure was sold. Young men would leave the relative security of home, family and work to fight for a common cause. They may have viewed it as an opportunity to see the world and step out from under parental authority. They didn't know then what we know now.

Biographers claim that Shackleton was an avid reader, which sparked his passion for adventure. Yet he didn't particularly distinguish himself as a scholar, and was said to be bored by his studies. He was quoted later as saying: "I never learned much geography at school."

Shackleton was restless at school and he was allowed to leave at 16 and go to sea. He opted to train for a life in the Merchant Navy. Not all his adventures were successful, but he had the ability to forge a great team. He was a born leader of men. He was sacrificial in the way he looked after his fellow explorers. He commanded their respect and devotion. He seems to me to have been an ordinary bloke who did extraordinary things.

I wonder whether my father was influenced by hearing about Shackleton's adventures when in 1926 he, too, left school at sixteen for a life in the Merchant Navy. He wanted to see the world. He needed an adventure. He too became a good leader.

A conversation with friends replays in my mind. We talked about what is written on the hearts of men. We considered what draws men to embark on daring exploits, where they allow themselves to be pushed to the limit and tested to see if they have what it takes. Every day we see competitiveness and a desire to succeed. This manifests itself in healthy and unhealthy ways. Is this the way men are wired? We compared that to the passiveness which we see in some men, those who seem resigned to lead a life of relative safety and security, with no sense of adventure at all.

> **They were willing to follow a man talking about a completely different kind of life**

What a surprise then to find that a number of seasoned fishermen respond to an invitation to leave their nets and follow a travelling preacher into an unknown future. They would be no strangers to danger or maritime adventures. But they left behind the work they had trained to do, their friends and family and all that was familiar. They were willing to follow a man talking about a completely different kind of life, treasure in heaven, and a role in establishing the kingdom of God on earth.

He must have been some guy to initially command their respect and later their devotion. He spent three years coaching them for a mission which would leave its mark on history. Then he handed the mission over to them. They in turn have handed it to us.

What justice can we fight for? What hope can we bring to desperate situations? What good news can we offer the poor? How can we release prisoners from darkness?

The lone ranger

John's Dad left home when he was nine years old and he didn't see much of him after that. Although his mum tried to make up for the lack of his father, as he grew up he quickly realised that he would need to figure out a lot of stuff on his own. He learned to fend for himself.

When I first met him he was a young teenager at a youth centre. He'd be there most Friday evenings and would often just sit on his own, listening to the music. He didn't appear to have many friends. I sat with him one time and he told me part of his story. He'd often take himself off on his own into the wild. Darkness didn't frighten him and he'd learned a thing or two about survival. It didn't faze him. Sometimes he would stay out all night, sleeping under the stars. The challenge and the discomfort were part of the attraction.

We occasionally went on camping trips. I noticed he was quick to adapt to circumstances. Unafraid, he would break away from the rest of us and scout the route ahead, flagging up potential problems. It was intimidating and annoying for the leaders because he seemed to know more than they did. He instinctively knew which direction to go when we were lost, and how to safely traverse swollen streams.

As he grew older he became more adventurous. During time off work he set up his own trips into wild places, taking minimal equipment and very little by way of back up. His preparation was thorough and his sense of direction unerring in an era when there was no GPS signal to rely on. Each time the challenge was tougher and more demanding. He was willing to forgo certain pleasures in life to fulfil his latest dream. He didn't get entangled in long term relationships or other people's projects. He was single-minded and determined to succeed.

When I was a lad I used to watch The Lone Ranger on the TV. As his name implies he was a loner too. He didn't seem to have any home or family. Not sure he even had a name. He drifted endlessly around the Wild West with his faithful horse Silver, fighting the bad guys, and protecting the vulnerable. Every now and then his Native American friend, Tonto, would appear out of nowhere to help him out of a tight situation. But who was behind that mask? No one ever got to know.

My friend John's sense of reckless adventure didn't translate well into work life. He wasn't strong on collaboration. He wasn't a team player. He would take enormous risks. He became overly ambitious. There was no accountability. And when a crisis came in his life he had no one close to turn to.

Solitude can be a good thing, sharpening the senses, getting closer to creation, revealing what is hidden in our hearts. Sadly, I think maybe John's lack of fatherly direction as he grew up pushed him too far down the road of being a loner. He had some great skills and lots of ambition, but found it really difficult to work with others.

 *... adventure is written on a man's heart, but there comes a point, doesn't there, when a man needs to settle, put down roots, find friendship, find love.*

Although adventure is written on a man's heart, there comes a point, doesn't there, when a man needs to settle, put down roots, find friendship, find love. There's an equally strong desire to establish a home, create a family, and be part of a community. Even if there are times when we feel we must pursue an adventure, we need that sense of belonging and security to return to.

Pioneers and settlers

Ken is a pioneer, a man on a mission. He was going to start something new. He confidently predicts significant growth in the first twelve months. The expected growth would in turn need resources – buildings, equipment and a passionate workforce committed to the vision.

Dave is a settler. His is a ten year plan, with more modest goals and more steady growth. He's no less willing to pioneer something new, but much prefers to put down a root and develop relationships, establish a sense of community, identity and belonging, and create security.

Both men have vision. Our world needs pioneers *and* settlers. Both are valuable. Both can be involved in a grand adventure.

All new ideas require pioneers to get them off the ground, people who are willing to take some risks and boldly go where none have been before. People who somehow manage not only to stop the merry-go-round, but also have the presence of mind to get off before it starts spinning round again. Pioneers have the courage to break free and head in a new direction with no guarantees of success.

But some pioneers follow their dream with or without the blessing of others. They leave everyone behind and are impossible to follow, preferring to be a free agent, not bound by accountabilities. They may seem unconcerned by the pressures others are enduring, because to get involved might deflect them from their vision. Pioneers can both inspire and frustrate us.

> **Our world needs pioneers and settlers. Both are valuable. Both can be involved in a grand adventure.**

We may also have come across settlers who are so rooted, enjoying the comfort of their immediate environment, that they lose sight of those outside the settled community. Weary travellers, who would love a sense of belonging, can feel excluded.

Perhaps there's something of the pioneer and the settler in us all.

Warning

I found these warnings on the back of a replacement mains adaptor for my laptop. I've read them a few times and still don't get either of them. What exactly are the hazards they are trying to flag up? Saying that something might not cause a problem isn't really a warning is it? So although there are warnings, they are unclear, and I'm not sure what to look out for.

Growing up I was aware that pursuing certain directions might result in an undesired consequence. Run into the road and you might be hit by a car; jump off the sea wall at high tide and you will probably drown. You could also argue that we all have some sort of built-in survival mechanism which might make us cautious in certain situations. But, apart from the Highway Code, many of the hazards in everyday life were never really communicated clearly, in a way that made sense to me.

Sure, there were a few voices proclaiming the evils of rock and roll and going to the pub, but with no adequate reason why either might be bad. Basically, anything which smacked of fun seemed to be frowned upon. But I loved watching live music. I didn't associate any danger with it. So, as a teenager, I went to a particular club to listen to the bands which played there. I was completely unaware that there was a drugs sub-culture centred on this venue. It never occurred to me to even think about it. Thankfully, I wasn't there on the night when the police raided the place and shut it down. Close call!

I'm conscious too, that during our formative years in particular, most of us rebel against everything. We don't automatically accept parental advice and frequently think we know it all. We often reject the acceptable behaviours of previous generations. We push the boundaries and find things out the hard way -by making mistakes. All that is fairly common.

Sometimes I hear other blokes talk about how their Dad used to say this or that. His words have lodged firmly in their memory. Sadly, my Dad checked out early from this planet when I was a teenager. I've not heard his voice speaking wisdom into my life when I've been unsure what to do. Conversations about what might constitute a good idea or a bad idea never happened. My Mum's protective fears for me might have influenced me more than my Dad's sense of adventure. So I've figured things out for myself and made many mistakes along the way.

But even way into adult life we might still make poor choices in the way we behave. What shapes our inner sense of what is right or wrong in our conduct and motives? How is that conscience shaped? What provides the inner strength or courage we need to make better choices? What influences the decisions we make? Is it nature or nurture, or both? Or is it something else? Does it come from inside us or from some external source? One definition of behaviour is: 'the response of a system or organism to various stimuli whether internal or external, conscious or sub-conscious, voluntary or involuntary'. Even though we know some actions will take us down a wrong road, why is it that sometimes we do it anyway? Are the behavioural choices we make influenced by our underlying beliefs, hopes and fears?

Whether or not the dangers written on the laptop charger were just poor translation by someone in China I don't know. But maybe there is some wisdom in there after all when it says *'This device must accept any interference received'*. Something seems to be affecting the way we think and react. Our 'device' is encountering interference, disrupting the way our lives were designed to function. Perhaps there is a sense in which we need to accept that 'interference' and learn how to deal with it.

Aragunt and legless

It was a strange world which I found myself in. Like stumbling through some Narnia wardrobe and finding myself in an adventure. My four year old grandson was directing. He was a character called Aragunt, and I was his trusty side kick, Legless. At least that's what I think he said. As so often with boys, the adventure quickly descended into fighting. Our eclectic mix of makeshift weapons included swords, a light sabre, bows and arrows and a BMW motorbike 'horse'.

Meanwhile, his eight year old brother was writing a sci-fi story. He cast himself as the hero who saves the day when his spaceship crash lands on a planet of unfriendly aliens. This particular homework assignment specified a twist in the tale. The crew were chased back to their spaceship and repaired it with magic stones. They fired up the rocket and the spaceship took off. But the hero was left behind as he engaged in an act of selfless bravery, fighting off the aliens to allow the others to escape. How would he get back home? We may never know.

Adventure and heroism are written on the heart of every young boy. He may not recognise it yet but he finds himself in the middle of a battle, a struggle between right and wrong, good guys and bad guys. What he may not realise is, although he is a hero, he has his own flaws and darkness. He will question again and again whether he has what it takes to be a real man and fulfil his destiny.

In teenage years and young adulthood the battles will continue. Subtle and persuasive enemies will endeavour to silence him, take him out, steal his true inheritance or force him to submit to a different authority and lose heart. The mythical adventures of childhood morph into X-box and YouTube. The realities of education, getting a job, and finding somewhere to live begin to weigh heavily. His lion heart may shrivel up when he learns that life is not a game which can be turned off and re-started. There are responsibilities to face. His roar may become a whimper.

Then one day he may hear again that ancient call. Will he be re-awakened and embark upon a dangerous mission in service of his fellow man? Not all will hear that inner voice for it comes initially as a whisper rather than a shout. Not many will want to re-join the battle when there is no obvious advantage, no personal gain or guarantee of victory. It may mean working behind enemy lines. Territory long since surrendered will take time to reclaim. Small victories will be hard won.

Just when I thought it was safe to step out of the wardrobe and back into reality, I was invited into another adventure. This time I would be Grandadalf, which I much preferred to being Legless.

beyond the banter

When was the last time you were invited to go on an adventure?

Even though we know some actions will take us down a wrong road, why is it that we do them anyway?

Do you think you are a Lone Ranger?

CHAPTER SEVEN

Photo: John Eastham Fraser

7 Influences

Blackpool rocks

Where do you go for a short break? I read somewhere that Blackpool is the UK's number one destination for a short break. It was probably in a publicity brochure put out by Blackpool Tourism. It certainly is popular for stag and hen weekends.

I lived there as a youngster and spent all my school days there. Blackpool has long been famous for its Tower, Golden Mile and illuminations. I used to play football with my friends on the beach opposite the Golden Mile, using the lifeboat house pillars as goal posts. In the Victorian and Edwardian era the resort was renowned for its bracing sea air. My recollection is the mixed aroma of hot dogs, candy floss, chips and donkey droppings. I don't think they do donkey rides anymore because the droppings constitute a health and safety hazard.

Families would stroll along the sand-strewn promenade dodging the trams, before descending the steps to find a suitable place to set up camp on the beach. In the shadow of the 518 feet high steel tower children would build sand castles and eat ice creams. Grandads rolled up their trousers and paddled, knotted handkerchief on head, and then returned to their striped corporation deck chairs. Mums dowsed their children with calamine lotion to protect them from the sun, but parents didn't often use sun protection themselves. Not surprisingly, they ended up as red as lobsters.

When I was ten my Dad used to take me to Bloomfield Road Football Ground. Blackpool Football Team were in the first division. The professional game was in its infancy and players played mainly for honour and hardly at all for money. Back home after the match we would tune in to the Sports Report on the radio and listen intently to the results and commentaries. It took over forty years for Blackpool FC to re-join the top flight teams in the Premiership, only to be relegated the following year. The expected boost to the town's tourist trade evaporated as quickly as it had appeared.

In the heyday of the 1950s and 60s three railway stations served the town. A massive influx of holiday makers poured in during the annual 'wakes weeks'. Especially feared would be those from Glasgow. The local paper would regularly report violence on the streets late at night, fuelled by excess alcohol. Sometimes there were knifings. It was an ugly place at night time, and only marginally better by day. The town was full of souvenir shops selling buckets and spades, tee-shirts and saucy postcards.

The story goes that in those days, on a typical summer Sunday morning in the town's three and a half thousand hotels and boarding houses, half a million eggs and two million rashers of bacon would be served. By midnight, two large herds of pigs would have been turned into bacon, sausages and pork pies for the tourists and forty acres of potatoes would have been turned into chips. In one summer season, over forty seven miles of hot dog sausages would be consumed. I think I may become a vegetarian.

Many things about Blackpool seem impressive. The tower is a triumph of Victorian steel engineering with a circus ring in the basement. There are several miles of sandy beach. The illuminations switch on in October and extend the season longer than other resorts. There are many amusement arcades and slot machines. The town has the dubious image of being labelled the Las Vegas of the UK. Many buildings on the promenade have impressive facades and when darkness falls strategic neon lighting adds a significant drama to their appearance.

Blackpool can be a fun place of live entertainment, night clubs, kiss me quick hats and generally outrageous behaviour. But behind the façade is another story. A transient workforce, a serious drug and homelessness problem, many people in debt and poverty. Rather like a film set, everything is not all it first appears to be.

How many of us have a façade which we hide behind? Behind it there could be heartache, illness, disappointment, disconnectedness, or cynicism. Sometimes we don't want anyone to know what's going on in our lives and the neon lights on the outside conveniently mask the darkness behind. But sometimes, as painful as it seems at the time, it's actually a good thing when the façade falls over, or the film set of our lives gets de-constructed. Because at that point we have a choice to either prop it all back up again or decide to be less secretive and more authentic.

> *... as painful as it seems at the time, it's actually a good thing when the façade falls over, or the film set of our lives gets de-constructed.*

Visiting friends in Blackpool is an occasional thing. It's less likely that I will take a short break there as I could watch Blackpool play football on the telly in the comfort of my own living room. Despite the tackiness, facades and neon lights I remember it fondly as the place where my spiritual journey began.

A lion or a poodle?

Every now and then something turns your world completely upside down. Everything you had come to know or to believe gets stood on its head. You come away feeling that the deepest longings, the biggest dreams, the greatest adventures, which had somehow got buried beneath the rubble of life's events, were being re-awakened and were straining to be unleashed.

Following a significant period of little or no real adventure in my life, and after a relationship breakdown, I took off for a break in Australia. I took two books with me. One was the obligatory travelogue by Bill Bryson. The other was Wild at Heart by John Eldredge. I was lost and confused, battle weary and exhausted, wounded and defeated. The events of life had overtaken the deep desires of my heart. Dreams were flattened; hopes were crushed. Like a survivor after an earthquake, I wandered aimlessly, unsure of anything anymore.

This was an event for men, real men, living in a real world. It was calling us to take a look in the mirror and check what we see.

Australia held the promise of adventure, sunshine and re-connection with an old friend who moved there in 1979. It proved to be the start of a significant shift in my thinking, and the beginnings of finding my heart again. That trip gave me back some self-esteem, restored some confidence, and renewed some hope. You can't dream dreams or look confidently into the future without first knowing some restoration of the heart.

Later that year I accepted an invitation from an old friend to attend a conference for men. There were Harley Davidson Bikes in the foyer of the main auditorium, and a circular reception desk, such as you would find in the best venues. The bookshop was in fact about 75% full of videos and CDs and only about 25% books. There was a wet-shave salon to one side; a multi-screen action video playing on one wall. The background music bordered on being intrusive. The auditorium itself seated around 2000 comfortably. For this event there were about 2,500 present. It was tight! It was full of male testosterone. As church events go it was very different!

This was an event for men, real men, living in a real world. It was calling us to take a look in the mirror and check what we see. What are we really like? What is influencing our character? What is dictating our values? Is there any evidence of the spirit of adventure? Or self-sacrifice? Or of overcoming for the sake of others? Or do we see a man who is half what we know deep inside we should be, who can rarely muster the energy to implement one new good habit, never mind engage with his life partner or children, or stand up for the poor or the weak or the wounded.

The opening meeting set the tone for the other four sessions, with a challenge as to whether we were lions or poodles. As a lion cub, had we unwittingly been brought up like domesticated, pampered poodles in a relatively sanitised and soft way? Were we compliant and safe rather than wild and dangerous?

I heard echoes of John Eldredge when he writes: "Christianity isn't a religion about going to Sunday School, hot pot suppers, being nice, holding car washes, sending our second-hand clothes off to charity – as good as those things might be. This is a world at war. Something large and immensely dangerous is unfolding all around us."

Tough or tender?

Imagine for a moment the atmosphere of a big sporting occasion, like say a rugby international. Men get excited, shouting their heads off, cheering their heroes. There's a unity in this, a solidarity of common purpose. It's loud and it's highly charged. The cheering is like a battle cry. The sound rings in your ears and the memories are written on your heart in the aftermath.

the thermostat in many churches is set in favour of feminine values and qualities such as love communication, beauty, relationships, support, nurture, feelings, and sharing.

Men also get excited at rock concerts, getting caught up in pounding rhythms and piercing lyrics. Men like the impressive sound and lighting rigs, and the instrumental excellence. Songs which have stirred their hearts are sung with every bit of passion and strength and volume they can muster, you clap and cheer and whistle and shout and dance and get excited.

This event was like that. The Lions theme was consolidated by a big plug for the book Why Men Hate Going To Church by David Murrow. His conclusions are based on well researched facts. He discovered that the thermostat in many churches is set in favour of feminine values and qualities such as love communication, beauty, relationships, support, nurture, feelings, and sharing. That's because on the whole women are the ones who show up. The more masculine interests of competence, efficiency, achievement, skill, and technology are largely missing from our church experience. Murrow claims that both sets of values are needed and the thermostat needs adjusting to maintain the balance.

I returned from that event determined not to settle for the comfortable and the comforting, and with a desire to find ways to allow the lion within to emerge. I will do it if only for the sake of my children. I don't want them to look back on my life in years to come and think of me only as a sensitive, gentle, mild-mannered, nice bloke. I don't want to leave them with the impression that faith is unimportant, that church is irrelevant and ineffective, that there is no spiritual dimension to life. I will make it my aim to make a difference to them and to others before it's too late.

4000 miles from Alaska

Thirty years ago I thought nothing of doing a full day's work before travelling 100 miles to a gig with the band in the evening. We would arrive back well after midnight, and still get up for work the next day. Nowadays turning out again after a busy day's work requires more effort.

It had been a wet winter's day. The sort of day when you just want to return to the shelter and comfort of all that's familiar. The more manly options of pioneering and scouting evaporate in the evening gloom. But I was tempted from the safe harbour of domestic comfort into the uncharted waters of Thornton, just north of Liverpool, by a presentation from David Murrow. This bloke had travelled four thousand miles from Alaska to give a talk. It would be rude not to turn up for that. Murrow came armed with in depth research, convincing statistics and an overriding passion to stimulate new thinking and reverse a trend which had been going for a couple of centuries. Murrow's book, Why Men Hate Going to Church, fuelled my need to write blogs for men.

So powerful was the message and so profound the impact, I subsequently bought ten copies to give away. I have spent most of my adult life as a church goer, with the majority of those years actively involved in trying to communicate relevantly to my generation, yet have missed something vital. My view was from the inside.

It was liberating to be given permission to question why men might be uncomfortable in a typical church, even a fairly lively church, where what is on offer would frequently include singing, talks, prayer meetings, bible studies, hugging, and sharing. Many men find such nurturing environments suffocating.

With hindsight the organisers of the David Murrow event may have chosen a different setting. The venue was a fairly feminine church environment with flowers and banners. This irony was not lost on me and it served well as a visual aid, reinforcing much of what Murrow had to say.

 *men and women are different, and the average un-churched man is like a fish out of water in the average church.*

His big point is that men and women are different, and the average un-churched man is like a fish out of water in the average church. Men find it hard to succeed in church because, on the whole, women are better at sharing, talking, listening, comforting, nurturing and learning. Men need things to be more factual, more inspiring, more visual, more purposeful, more technological, more adventurous, and teaching needs to be more concise and more relevant to grab their attention and motivate their lives.

Murrow's presentation lasted thirty five minutes. Initially, I felt cheated, but the questions went on for well over an hour after, as he settled fears about a 'macho', emotion-free culture, appealing instead for a restoration of balance rather than a tipping of the scales towards men. Most delegates seemed fired up and ready to rethink their strategy.

I came away from the meeting with renewed enthusiasm to read the book again; to continue to be part of the current pioneering moves to make faith more relevant for men; to deepen my own spirituality and not get blown off course or settle for being a spectator; and to link up with others who want to centre their lives on God and find destiny and purpose.

Why Men Hate Going to Church is written by David Murrow and published by Nelson Books.

An elaborate fig leaf

"We are not what we were meant to be, desperately afraid of exposure. Terrified of being seen for what we are and are not, we have run off into the bushes. We hide in our office, at the gym, behind the newspaper, and mostly behind our personality. Most of what you encounter when you meet a man is a facade, an elaborate fig leaf, a brilliant disguise".
Extract from Wild at Heart by John Eldredge.

The author, John Eldredge, has greatly influenced my thinking. He makes some excellent points about the way we hide behind things.

Like many blokes, I have different facets which can be seen depending on where your viewpoint is. People at work may see my ambition; my family may see my kindness and my faults; my musician friends may see my creativity. But how much of what people see is the real me, and how much is a façade?

> *I'm more aware than ever before that I need to live a life with more positive values, with some sense of destiny, and with a greater call to make a difference in whatever time I have left.*

There have been times when I've been afraid to voice my real thoughts and was too quick to go with the majority. In some seasons I've been too pre-occupied with my own battles to want to rescue others. Other times I've been too passive to engage with the key people in my life, especially when the going gets tough.

I'm not alone. Many blokes I meet live their lives with this confusion. It's hard to work out who the real person is. But sometimes we get to a place where the sheer effort of keeping up an appearance is so exhausting that we just have to be real. And that takes courage.

These days I listen more to my heart, that still, small voice inside, which in the past has been drowned out by other voices. I'm more aware than ever before that I need to live a life with more positive values, with some sense of destiny, and with a greater call to make a difference in whatever time I have left.

The winter years

Honour and enjoy your creator while you're still young. Before the years take their toll and your vigour wanes. Before your vision dims and the world blurs and the winter years keep you close to the fire.
(Eugene H Peterson - The Message)

My Mum died peacefully in hospital aged 94. The family gathered round her bedside. We heard her take that final breath. It was exactly how she would have wanted it. Her funeral was as many funerals are, bitter and sweet. The sting of loss brings bitter, crushing sadness. The release of a weary soul brings sweet comfort.

Mum loved a good laugh. On many family photos she is laughing. She never seemed to burden us with any of the things that could have made her miserable. She told us that my Dad used to call her 'Min'. Apparently this was a reference to Mini-Ha-Ha in the book Hiawatha, an epic love poem written by Henry Longfellow in 1855. Hiawatha falls in love with Mini Ha Ha, whose name meant laughing water. So Dad's nick name for her accurately captured Mum's fun nature.

Reflecting on Mum's life and who she was, has helped me to understand that it's not what you know, what you've achieved, your net worth, or how many Facebook friends you have which really matters. It's who you are in your heart.

Mum left school with a good report. But beyond that there was no college or further education other than the University of Life. She never learned to swim, ride a bike, or drive a car. She struggled with most gadgets, especially in later life. The winter years kept her close to the fire as her world grew smaller. Yet she had profound wisdom and insight, stemming from her unshakeable faith in her creator.

As well as being wise, I think Mum was also inspirational and influential. In one sense she wasn't a high achiever. She had no high profile or status or financial power. She lived a relatively simple life. She wasn't well travelled. Yet, all of us in the family, and the many friends she made through her long life, felt her gentle influence. We were inspired by her determination, and encouraged by her unconditional love. How is it that even in her final years someone who seemed so small and fragile could still have so much influence?

All of this makes me wonder what others will make of my life when my turn comes.

I don't know how you would define a successful life, but Ralph Waldo Emmerson said this: "To know that even one life has breathed easier because you have lived, this is to have succeeded." On that basis I reckon my Mum's life was a massive success.

> *... it's not what you know, what you've achieved, your net worth, or how many Facebook friends you have which really matters. It's who you are in your heart.*

beyond the banter

What shapes your inner sense of what is right or wrong?

What provides the inner strength or courage you need to make better choices?

What books, people or events have shaped your thinking?

CHAPTER EIGHT

8 Seasons

A winter's tale

Amid the clamour of consumerism, David Essex singing 'It's only a winter's tale' stopped me in my tracks in the middle of the supermarket. I have no idea why. I don't know the rest of the lyrics, only the title. It's not even one of my favourites. Did the music evoke memories from the deepest recesses of my mind? Salvation Army bands have a similar effect at this time of year. Is it pure nostalgia? It all adds to the poignancy of the season.

It seems to me that the origins of the festive season are increasingly being obscured by the tinsel and trappings. The consumer world promotes a celebration of a different kind, requiring us to gaze in wonder at the latest toys and gadgets and have our best Christmas ever.

For me the Christmas story isn't 'only a winter's tale.' It's a tale of cosmic significance. The King of Heaven breaks into our earthly existence in Roman occupied Palestine in a totally unexpected way. He arrives as a baby to a trusting Mum and an embarrassed step-Dad.

Shepherds watching their flocks by night, were visited by angelic beings, who directed them to a stable in Bethlehem. There they saw a new born baby. Wise men also made a journey from a faraway country to see the baby. Personally, I reckon between them, those blokes had many unspoken questions.

Not much is recorded as the baby grew through childhood to manhood, developing carpentry skills in the family business. But at the age of thirty, he began to fulfil a destiny foretold by prophets hundreds of years earlier. He was compassionate with those whose lives were impacted by poverty, oppression and sickness.

He became known for his teaching, his miracle working and his faith. He challenged the religious leaders of his day as to the authenticity of their beliefs. He talked about the Kingdom of God. His three year public life ended in what seemed like a cruel, untimely death, and a disputed resurrection.

I believe His life is a historical fact. He's had a huge impact, influencing the lives of individual men, women and children world-wide to this day. Yet his birth, public life and his death were all surrounded in controversy.

So as I hear the sound of David Essex singing his familiar Christmas anthem, I pray that, despite the increasing secularisation of Christmas, our children and, in time, their children might not lose sight of the reason for the season, and approach the Christmas story with honest questions, because it's so much more than a winter's tale.

Last Christmas

Wham's Christmas hit plays whilst we're out shopping. I'm reminded that last Christmas the Post Office, who normally issue special stamps to denote the religious festival, produced two alternatives, presumably in the interest of equality. One had no religious significance and the other was a Madonna and Child design. However, I'm told that only the non-religious ones were offered over the counter. The religious one had to be requested. Apparently they were testing public demand for religious stamps at Christmas, with a view to abandoning them altogether. So, not exactly a fair test of public opinion, if both are not equally available.

The powers that be have for a number of years in many places effectively squeezed out of their agenda the 'reason for the season' in an attempt to be multi-cultural, inclusive and respectful to people of all faiths and none. Yet, irrespective of beliefs, most countries in the world have strong traditions, and the re-telling of the Christmas story has become part of the UK tradition.

A significant chunk of the population find themselves attending nativity plays, Christmas fairs, midnight communion services, Christingle and carol services.

Festive events can really forge community, strengthen cohesion and deepen friendships. There is also a significant emphasis on peace and goodwill to all, and a greater focus on looking out for the poor and disadvantaged. UK society seems to acknowledge that Christmas is a major holiday and a time when extended families get together.

> *Festive events can really forge community, strengthen cohesion and deepen friendships.*

The trouble is the whole thing has become hijacked by an excess of consumerism, fuelled by advertising. Many people are uncomfortable with this, can't really afford it, generally whinge about it, but go along with it anyway. In some respects our culture has taken church traditions and morphed them into materialistic expressions.

Faith communities aren't wholly innocent when it comes to hijacking either! Throughout history many secular celebrations and traditions have been transformed into religious events, presumably with a view to encouraging a fresh understanding of faith. In the midst of this, the poor are still starving, the homeless are still without shelter and more people than I feel comfortable thinking about are lonely and excluded.

Last year faith communities in some towns and cities took Christmas to the people and held out-door multi-venue, multi-media cultural events. Meanwhile, thousands sidestepped the whole thing and headed for the pub or the Costa Del Sol.

So how will I be spending this Christmas? I hope that I will be keeping some old traditions and starting some new ones. I'll be planning to see family and friends and I'll be looking for authenticity and relevance in expressions of Christmas both in the church and in the community. I'll be thankful that I have life and health and strength, a roof over my head and a choice over how I celebrate the festival. Most of all, I hope that I will maintain a connection with Christmas tradition and not allow it to be squeezed out of the agenda.

Awe and wonder

As each New Year commences there are images in the media of the New Year's Eve celebrations and the countdown to midnight. This year there were scenes from all around the world with huge crowds looking skywards, some with hands raised in joy, others dancing in celebration. Others were weeping with emotion.

For some no doubt this was a chance to be part of a massive celebration. For some a time to forget the troubles of the past year and show some optimism for the future. Some almost conveyed a sense of worship. But these photographs were not of any conventional worship event. 'Worshippers' in cities across the globe watched in awe and wonder at impressive firework displays to mark the occasion.

In stark contrast, I saw an image of a Palestinian woman also with arms outstretched but her tears were not of joy but of grief. She was in mourning after an Israeli air strike had destroyed her house. Surrounded by rubble and devastation, she looked to the sky as if to ask why? Will there ever be an end to violence and suffering?

We live in a world where mourning is never far from celebration. Despair casts a shadow over hope. One man's captivity tempers another's freedom. In the midst of life is death.

Here in the UK, I watched from a first floor window at midnight as rockets soared and exploded. Chinese lanterns rose rather more serenely in the moonlit sky taking with them unspoken hopes and prayers for the year ahead.

Meanwhile, London's New Year 'worship' event resounded to the sights and sounds of a firework display along the River Thames. The overall cost of the event was £1.9 million which included music performances, staffing, security and around £250,000 worth of fireworks. The display lasted about twelve minutes and the smoke rose like incense in the night sky.

We live in a world where mourning is never far from celebration. Despair casts a shadow over hope. One man's captivity tempers another's freedom.

beyond the banter

Is it difficult to avoid consumerism at Christmas?

What memories does Christmas awaken?

How can Christmas forge a sense of community?

CHAPTER NINE

9 Faith

Cash in the attic

While watching the telly I noticed that the main references to Easter, were shoehorned in between The Malaysian Grand Prix and an episode of Cash in the Attic. Another time Easter was eclipsed between a repeat of Match of the Day and Escape to the Country. An Anglican cathedral service and a message from the Pope were the key components.

Of course this doesn't tell the whole story. But for me, it's a stark reminder that in the UK we seem to be living in a largely secular society. Yet many claim to have faith in God, or at least acknowledge there is some higher power at work, even if they don't gather in a place of worship that often. Evidently attendance at cathedrals is on the increase, and there are some 'new breed' churches which are bucking the trend and are immensely popular with vast congregations.

There are some faithful people in UK churches. In a puzzling world many are trying to keep that personal connection with their creator alive. Some are working hard to include young people, especially their own children and grandchildren. They are connecting with others and serving their community. Resources are limited but they serve with all of their energy and enthusiasm.

We in the UK have more than many in the world. Yet, the more stuff we have, the more it seems we fear the loss of it. Indeed, in developing but less well-off places like India, Africa and South America, there is an explosion of faith. Perhaps poverty concentrates the mind and brings clarity. The TV programme 'Cash in the Attic' awakens the vague feeling that there's something up there of great value, though long forgotten. I would be excited to discover cash in my own attic! But for now I'm seeking a different kind of treasure. One, though long forgotten by many, is of great value to me.

> *... I'm seeking a different kind of treasure.*

Faith

For many, having a faith, answers some of their deepest questions and gives meaning to why we're on the planet. Many find it difficult to believe that the very complex design of everything in nature, and indeed the human body, could have happened by chance. Creation is wild, unpredictable and mysterious. Despite man's best efforts to explain everything through science, many believe in something beyond themselves.

In some religions, faith is tied into everyday life. It's part of the culture and tradition, sometimes requiring observance several times each day. Elsewhere, religion and state seem intertwined and it seems to me that there is little room for freedom of belief. Yet other expressions are militant and political, often leading to violence.

I'm most uncomfortable with extremist and fundamentalist views, whatever religion they emanate from. Radical preaching, dogmatic statements, and things which exclude others in some way, leave me troubled and uneasy.

Sometimes it can be tricky, for men in particular, to fit into a faith community. Old school preaching produces some results, but mainly by inducing guilt and fear. Getting people into heaven is the primary objective, as opposed to loving your neighbour in the here and now. A loud, shouty challenge can come across as macho and insensitive.

In stark contrast, some expressions of faith proclaim such a weak call that men don't hear it, and can't respect it. There's too much reflection and not enough action. Too much 'tender' and not enough 'tough'. As

David Murrow points out in his book 'Why Men Hate Going To Church', the leadership in many churches set the thermostat for those who show up most - women and children. The environment can be too tame for men who prefer challenge and adventure.

And yet elsewhere, the expression of faith might be entirely emotional, with a call for only a heartfelt response, rather than an intellectual one. When rational thinking is dismissed involvement can quickly become out of balance. When self-realisation permanently out ranks the needs of others, thinking can become intense and unhealthy.

'New breed' churches have made their mark. Here, droves of young people are attracted by the high energy, concert style of presentation with motivational talks. Many of these expressions have cleared the clutter of religious jargon and protocols. They are relevant and more inclusive of the majority of people who have no understanding of traditional church. All of which is long overdue.

> *I count myself among the many who have, for a season, found comfort, shelter and friendship within the walls of a church. But is there more to church than refuge?*

Some men need a cause to commit to – what John Eldredge describes as 'A battle to fight'. They secretly long for a challenge that will galvanise their strength for positive action. Instead, many men have experienced a nagging, unspoken pressure to conform. They've been urged to play safe, stay home and grow up.

Faith communities can and do offer secure refuge and boundless compassion for the wounded and broken. And I count myself among the many who have, for a season, found comfort, shelter and friendship within the walls of a church. But is there more to church than refuge?

Grave news

From time to time I visit Hawkshead Hill, a small village in the Lake District National Park, UK. An ancient burial ground is nestled in the garden of the Baptist Chapel. The writer, William Wordsworth, once paid a visit. He had this to say:

"The ground is humbly fenced and not a tree to dignify or adorn it. But among this little company of graves, how much mortal weariness is laid to rest, how many anxieties are stilled, what fearful apprehensions removed forever."

Wordsworth couldn't have imagined that 200 years later, in a time of global insecurity, his words would still echo. As I sat briefly in that small, ancient graveyard, I reflected on my own 'mortal weariness', 'many anxieties' and 'fearful apprehensions', and enjoyed some moments of rest and stillness. I concluded that compared to many people in the world today I have a lot to be thankful for. Not everyone has the luxury of rest and stillness.

The words of David in Psalm 23 come to mind. 'You serve me a six course dinner right in front of my enemies.' The Message 23:5.

David was a man who knew much about battles. If anyone could claim to be battle weary it would be him. Yet, when surrounded by enemies, and facing great danger, he heard God say 'stop and rest; enjoy the feast; enjoy the green pastures, the still waters. Enjoy comfort and rest for the soul'. The result? Same situation, new point of view.

The challenge is to remain hopeful despite the circumstances. The present is what we have to deal with. We don't know what lies ahead. Faith is being sure of what we hope for and certain of what we do not see.

Faith is being sure of what we hope for and certain of what we do not see.

Hebrews 12:1 Good News Bible

Lost soul

Language evolves over time and our understanding of words needs to be adjusted to take account of new meanings. When I was younger 'lost souls' had a rather ghoulish, scary connotation. 'Soul winning' was about finger-wagging preaching which usually turned people off. I was never very comfortable with either.

I understand its meaning better now. In conflict zones around the world we have heard talk of the political battle for the soul of the nation; for the hearts and minds of the people. Soul music could be described as something which touches our innermost thoughts and feelings.

For me, this seems to more accurately reflect what our soul is. It's who we really are; it's what we believe; it's our core values; it's the centre of our true emotions. Winning souls, therefore, seems to be more about building confidence and trust with people to enable points of view to be shared without fear of judgement, condemnation or rejection. It's about creating a culture of acceptance and belonging.

I had hit what can only be described as a brick wall. Ok, it's an exaggeration to describe certain tasks as 'soul destroying', but there are occasions when it's pretty close to the mark. An on-going situation can feel as though it's slowly eroding our energy, enthusiasm and creativity. This is how it felt. Mind numbing, meaningless activity. The only upside was I got paid for it.

But to be honest, I valued my sanity more than the money. It wasn't my chosen career path, but it was all that was available. As I scoured jobs online, there was very little else out there which might offer more hope in either the fulfilment or the funding department. I came home each night feeling like I was losing my soul.

The erosion is subtle and we never see the crash coming. It's like the pictures we may have seen of coastal erosion. Day after day the sea batters the headland, then one day the cliff collapses onto the beach below. Sometimes houses are lost; sometimes lives are lost; sometimes everything is lost.

> *When we stay too long in something which is soul destroying our very essence can be undermined.*

When we stay too long in something which is soul destroying our very essence can be undermined. To feel you're in a soul destroying situation is dangerous. If we have the option, we must get out before the ground crumbles beneath our feet.

Myths and legends

A friend invited me along to see the latest Hobbit film. It's the sort of film which is more appealing to men than to women. Men love myths, legends and epic stories of adventure where good triumphs over evil. They hold a strange fascination for many of us.

We duly met at the cinema only to find that the schedule had been changed and the Hobbit film wasn't showing that afternoon. Nor anywhere else. His 'Plan B' suggestion was to go ten pin bowling. Having only played occasionally, the last time being ten years previous, I was a little rusty!

However, among the many rounds where I didn't get a strike at all, I had one when I got four strikes in a row! I knew three in a row and you were a 'turkey', but never before had I heard of anyone getting four. Personally, I'd never even had three! So I was unprepared for the declaration which came up on the screen that I was a 'four-bagger'. To me at least it was a story of epic proportions, albeit a short one.

Is there an epic struggle going on in our lives? Are our stories set within a much bigger story which is still unfolding? Many people have some consciousness of good and evil. We're aware of the cruelty to innocent people and of the need for justice and truth. We understand darkness and light. It seems intrinsic to our human nature. There can be a strange fascination with the darkness, and the unwary can easily get drawn into it. Hidden dangers exist there. We go through a door out of curiosity. The door slams and there's no handle on the inside.

Is it possible to draw on God's help? Can he reverse our tendency to hide in caves and dwell on our failures? Can He give courage to strengthen us? Can we listen to his affirmation and encouragement and replace our lethargy and isolation with a greater desire to be part of that epic story?

> *There can be a strange fascination with the darkness, and the unwary can easily get drawn into it.*

Winning and losing

Eric Lyddell was the son of a Chinese Missionary who discovered that he was blessed with a gift of running very fast. He felt called to honour God by competing in the 1924 Olympic Games held in Paris. But despite pressure from other athlete's and even royalty, he was uncomfortable about running on a Sunday, and he was on the verge of withdrawing from the competition. The popular film, Chariots of Fire, was based on Lyddell's story.

Men will identify with his competitive streak. The importance of winning is impressed on us from an early age. For many of us life is about winning or losing. Despite the courageous efforts of some to promote equality and less discrimination, society seems to value and celebrate winners and dismiss the losers.

Our victories and defeats can impact how we feel and how we believe others perceive us. Our own need to compete and win can be lived out and expressed in our support for a football team. My seven-year-old grandson is a keen football supporter. When I ask him how his team did at the weekend, the answer is written all over his face. In that context, winning is a mood setter. Whole communities are affected by the victories and defeats of their local football team.

When the UK won gold medals day after day in the 2012 and 2016 Olympics, you could sense the mood of the population shift. It was something to be proud of in a world where there was little else to celebrate. Expectation grew for further success. National pride was restored for a while.

No one enjoys losing but the desire to win seems hard wired in some blokes. Which can be a good thing. Winning requires perseverance and determination. Those are good qualities. But when winning becomes all-consuming, and is at the expense of others, it's not so a good. Competition in business may mean expansion for one company but redundancies elsewhere. A lot of hurt has been caused by the desire to be top dog.

Eric Lyddell was competitive; he was also a man of faith. He somehow achieved that elusive balance of competing, with some determination, and yet remaining true to his faith. A remarkable accomplishment in my opinion.

Running on empty

In the 1970s Jackson Browne had great success with his song 'Running on Empty'. I listened to it again recently as a friend of mine said he felt like he was running on empty. He had nothing left in the reserve tank. He felt his life was on hold and had been for some time.

Is this a picture you recognise in someone you know, or indeed, would it describe what you feel right now? It's easy in times like that to feel like giving up and withdrawing from the battle front.

Sometimes we do need to withdraw, rest awhile, get some balance back into our lives and some perspective on our problems. Such times of quiet give us chance to listen to our hearts. But to be entirely on our own can be dangerous.

At other times we just don't have the strength to raise the shield of faith and protect ourselves from all that life would throw at us. At times like that it's very easy to back away from all our familiar sources of help and encouragement.

In those moments we need to remind ourselves that the enemy of our souls has accomplished his objective if he can isolate and immobilise us. It would be much better to gather some friends around us rather than battle on alone. A sense of belonging and community is good, especially when we're running on empty.

beyond the banter

How important is faith in your life?

Are faith communities like hospitals, primarily places for the wounded?

Where do you find places of refuge?

CHAPTER TEN

10 Hope

Worry

When news broke of the Australian government being warned of a potential terrorist attack I remember my anxiety. My daughter was there on holiday. Her next stop was Thailand, an area which had been devastated by a tsunami, less than a year previously. As her father, I was worried.

Then there were six nights of rioting in Paris with buses and buildings set on fire. Police were on the streets with full riot gear and rubber bullets. The local newspaper dropped through my letterbox. Stories of violence troubled me. Was it like this when I was growing up?

My father died aged 56 when I was 17. As I clocked up my own 56 years on the planet, I seemed suddenly to be faced with a general worry about health issues, which had not been the norm for me to date.

We are surrounded by potentially fearful situations. The outcome is often beyond our control. We can't influence terrorist activity or an explosion of social unrest. We can't guarantee that we will be healthy or that our children will suffer no pain in life. It's not uncommon to experience some level of worry.

We are surrounded by potentially fearful situations. The outcome is often beyond our control.

Before a scheduled injection for a painful shoulder, colleagues kindly shared their own medical experiences in some detail. This greatly enhanced my impression of how painful the process would be. In the event, I didn't feel much pain, either from the injection, or afterwards, but my anxiety was reinforced by hearing the views of others.

The heart can endure relationship breakdown and loss of friendship. It can nurse feelings of deep disappointment because of the way others have devalued or used us. There may be deep, lingering, regrets over wrong decisions.

We anxiously project a worrying situation to a worst-case scenario, in a bid to protect ourselves from further wounds. But when we focus only on the negatives around us, our imagination can create a picture, which is often far worse than the reality.

We're all doomed

In the nineteen-eighties, there was a popular sit-com, 'Dad's Army', based on the activities of the Home Guard during the Second World War. The strengths and weaknesses in many of the characters were readily identifiable, both in myself and others. Each week Captain Mainwaring had the almost impossible task of shaping that disparate bunch of volunteers into an effective platoon. Like millions of viewers, I loved the variety of personalities portrayed, and took great delight in watching their blunders unfold from a safe distance.

It was my namesake, Fraser, who dramatically delivered the wide-eyed catch phrase "We're all doomed!" The circumstances of life can come against us and immobilise us. Storms can arise and shipwreck our hopes and dreams, leaving us with a sense of failure and confusion, wondering where we go from here. Some men take refuge in pursuits which are not helpful, playing computer games late into the night, flirting with addictive web sites, pursuing inappropriate liaisons with the opposite sex, drowning sorrows down at the pub or finding relief in drugs. At best all these escapes can offer is temporary respite from life's pressures. At worst, they increase the likelihood of relationship breakdown, deeper entrapment and yet more feelings of failure to deal with.

As I look out across the landscape of my own life there have been seasons of success and hope. And yet, running right alongside that, there have been times of failure and despair in other areas.

As I look out across the landscape of my own life there have been seasons of success and hope. And yet, running right alongside that, there have been times of failure and despair, in other areas.

But shouldn't we be living purposefully - more by design than by default? If we just drift through life, are we opting to live out our days with disappointment? Do we want to leave the planet regretting our failures, or would it be better to leave a legacy in the lives of others? If we opt for the former, then it may be that Fraser was right, and we are all doomed.

Emotional souvenirs

I've often brought home a souvenir when I've been on holiday. Usually a reminder of a happy time. Some people have particular souvenirs they look for. It may be unusual bottles, pottery, mugs or tea spoons. Sometimes pebbles or driftwood gathered from a beach can re-create the sights, sounds and aromas of the seaside. Photographs make great souvenirs. Each one prompting a memory.

I was flicking idly through a Sunday magazine recently when I came across a phrase I hadn't seen before - Emotional Souvenirs. I'd heard of emotional baggage (I have plenty), emotional insecurity (not unknown), emotional scars (yep, got some), and emotional wreck (have been on occasions). But until recently I'd never heard anyone talk about emotional souvenirs.

No matter what our belief system, there will always be things in life which we don't understand and cannot change. Sometimes we have to shift our viewpoint and look at these things from a different perspective. We can come away with some emotional souvenirs. Things which, rather than remind us of disaster or crisis, offer hope for the future.

> *No matter what our belief system, there will always be things in life which we don't understand and cannot change.*

Silent acceptance

I'm in touch with a number of men who feel that life isn't working out as hoped. That may be in the area of relationships, jobs, achievement or faith. I also meet many young men in prison for whom life has definitely gone pear-shaped. They are wounded and in need of help to restore and rebuild their lives with greater integrity and wholeness in body, mind and spirit. For now though, they seem subdued and battle weary.

You could say that some men are missing in action. A few have risked further humiliation by tentatively waving a white flag. That's not an easy thing to do - to admit defeat or failure - but it's a starting point.

> *... nowadays as I try to focus on others rather than myself, I feel a greater sense of identity, destiny, purpose and calling.*

I believe there are many more out there, silently accepting defeat. Like a forgotten army they are pinned down, hoping for rescue, but feeling that they should battle on and not ask for help. Still others may have good intentions to change behaviours which they know are not helping them, but they choose to stay in the same suffocating or negative environment and just keep repeating what they've always done. Each time they hope for a different result but wind up in a mess again.

Everyone experiences ups and downs in life. I would love to have been chosen for a mission or consulted for my expertise but more often I've been made redundant and de-valued. Like many men, I've hoped for a Band of Brothers, but more often found myself wandering 'behind enemy lines' alone. But nowadays, as I try to focus on others rather than myself, I feel a greater sense of identity, destiny, purpose and calling.

The big blag

Some men want to be heroes or to be looked up to as a leader who inspires others. Some men thrive on a sense of achievement, loving the challenge of finding a way through an impossible situation. But some heroes turn out to be flawed, blagging their way into positions of influence, or intent on their own agenda.

Paul was a man like that. He was punching above his weight when he applied for his current job. Yes, he had some skills to offer, and a good sense of humour. But he was the sort of guy who 'Googled' everything – even while he was on the phone – pretending to the caller that he knew what he was talking about. He also drew extensively on the knowledge of others in his team.

Because he was funny and personable they freely and willingly offered their experience, only to find out later that he had passed their ideas off as his own, and gained favour with the hierarchy for himself.

For some, like Paul, it's all about proving that they have what it takes. But when their human frailty is exposed, they quickly lose respect and it leaves considerable reluctance in their colleagues to offer help. People hesitate to commit to a man who blags his way through life, for fear of further disappointment and association with failure.

Other men project an image of self-sufficiency. They would have us believe they are able to survive the worst excesses of deprivation and extremes of temperature. Such men think they can navigate their way to anywhere using their built-in GPS sense of direction, surviving on a diet of dubious wild life. They feel only an occasional need to refer to a map or other people. What are they trying to prove?

There may be within all men the faint echo of an ancient call to be a hunter-gatherer in the wild. However, the majority live fairly sanitised lives and would be lost without smart phones and creature comforts, myself included. Not many of us head off into the wilderness just to be. But the vast landscapes of wild places can evaporate all falseness, blagging and delusion, like early morning dew. There's no hiding place for the soul. The beauty of creation washes over the heart, bringing honest restoration.

> *But the vast landscapes of wild places can evaporate all falseness, blagging and delusion, like early morning dew.*

Wonders of the universe

While watching the sun rise one morning I remembered that the sun wasn't really rising. The earth was turning.

The effect was still the same. It was still a wonder. A new dawn and a new day were unfolding, and I took ten minutes out to watch it.

Not long after, I watched a couple of 'Wonders of the Universe' programmes presented by Professor Brian Cox. It was mind boggling stuff with timescales, temperatures and distances I couldn't begin to comprehend. He did his best to explain complex theories in layman's terms. For him, science had to explain everything.

Although I do like to have some idea how things work, I'm quite happy living with a level of uncertainty and mystery in life. I don't really need to know everything.
When the tsunami and radiation scare hit Japan my mind was totally boggled. There was death, destruction and heartache on a monumental scale. How heart breaking to see homes and communities swept away, lives shattered, families grieving for lost relatives. My insecurities seem minute in comparison.

Every day we live carries a potential for highs and lows, happiness and disappointment, fulfilment or frustration. Every day has opportunities to make things better or to make things worse. So when I see tragedies I can't begin to comprehend, watching a sunrise helps dissolve my own small fears and bring a new ray of hope.

Whistling in the dark

A friend of mine went to a concert at his local community centre where one of the performers was the world champion whistler. I didn't even know there was a competition for such a thing. He was very impressed!

Apparently this guy could whistle the most complicated tunes.

I don't often hear people whistling these days. One of the things I remember about my dad was that he used to whistle. My mum said it was a sign that he was contented. But whistling in the dark is the exact opposite, and has more to do with apprehension than happiness.

When a colleague lost his father, suddenly and prematurely, in his mid-fifties, he described to me the shock and the unpredictable emotions which surfaced without warning like a sub-marine. He shared the difficulties of being a support to his mum, his brothers and sisters, his wife, and his kids all at the same time. He felt like he had to suspend his own grief until later. At work he put a brave face on. He was whistling in the dark.

I appreciated his honesty. Men don't often show such openness and share stuff like that. I shared briefly with him my own experience of bereavement and bought him a copy of a really helpful book on the subject of living with bereavement.

How many of us are whistling in the dark? Putting on a brave face? Unsure of what might happen next? There are times when it helps to admit that we can neither control or fix everything that life throws at us. In times like these others can lighten our darkness.

beyond the banter

Can the wonder of the natural world diminish worry?

Has hope ever helped you through a difficult season?

What are you hoping for in this season of your life?

Big Questions

What justice can we fight for?

What hope can we bring to desperate situations?

What good news can we offer the poor?

How can we release prisoners from darkness?

men's groups

> "If you want to walk fast, walk alone.
>
> If you want to walk far, walk together.
>
> African saying.

Men's Groups

A conversation about life and faith

It all began with a curry. Myself, and two blokes who attended the same church Life Group, took the opportunity to meet up while the girls were at a ladies only evening. We had a great night with great curry, great conversation and a couple of beers. But more than that, in many ways I felt it was remarkably different from our usual Life Group meeting. The dynamics were different. The conversation was different. The emphasis was different.

We bantered, yes. We discussed football and gadgets and work and curry, yes. Banter is a kind of modern day man's survival tool – a socially acceptable way of determining if someone is a friend or enemy. Leap frog over this step and a man is never quite sure whether the other person is 'for' or 'against' him. If on some level, a man decides that the other person is 'against' him, the drawbridge comes up. The banter may continue, but nothing significant is revealed.

As we engaged in the verbal sparring of casual male banter we began to relax, we began to feel at ease with each other, and all our inner competitiveness, blag and blather evaporated. Then something quite astonishing happened; we bravely ventured beyond the banter. Just a little bit. But we went there.

In those moments we connected in a way we had never quite achieved in a mixed company setting. My idea for a regular bloke's Life Group was born. In the first year membership grew from two to sixteen. The contact list has since grown to over 60 men who are interested in our monthly breakfast for blokes. We've bantered. We've laughed. We've become true friends. We've gone beyond the banter many, many times.

Long before starting the group I researched men's ministry in depth, attended conferences and read everything I could get my hands on. For many years I've worked alongside prison chaplains with male offenders in prison. More recently I became Christian Vision for Men (CVM) Regional Director England (North West). Many of the resources which have influenced and fuelled my current thinking are outlined in the next section. My own questions and ideas, which are expressed here, have been thoroughly road tested in the Life Group for Blokes which I've been running.

WORSHIP FOR BLOKES

Men readily sing their lungs out in a stadium, but can clam up in church. They will freely roar for their sporting hero with total abandonment, but can freeze at the invitation to sing for God. In a stadium they will wave their arms, and sway and rock shoulder to shoulder with their mates without the slightest hint of embarrassment. But then squirm uncomfortably or stand rigid in the presence of their God, robbed of the transforming power of worship.

Clearly, clearly, something is seriously, seriously wrong here.

As a worship leader and singer-songwriter, kindly described by Cross Rhythms as a veteran, I now realise that for a season, I may have contributed to this problem. During my many outreach years I observed that my music was relevant and sing-able for both genders. But then as I settled into church life there was a shift and I developed a sort of 'blokes blindness'. I was having a great time and I loved being part of some great bands! There was a definite trend to romanticise worship songs, and as an old romantic myself, I just couldn't see how your average bloke might struggle with that.

These days I'm intensely aware of how men experience church and worship music. I feel my current approach is more intelligible to those with little or no history of doing church. The worship songs I use in the Men's Group have dynamic, strong rhythms which men can follow, they fall in a musical range which isn't too high, can be comfortably sung with gusto by the average male voice, and the lyrics don't demand the mental gymnastics required for romantic declarations of love.

The acid test of an all-inclusive worship song is to observe men singing. If they dip out for a line or a word, either the lyrics are too girly or the notes are too high!

In addition, I outlined the following principles when the group began. So far they have worked well:

- ✓ It's a conversation about life and faith, rather than a seminar.

- ✓ It's not a Bible study, although we will keep things rooted in scripture.

- ✓ It's not a social club, though we will meet socially from time to time.

- ✓ We're not debating or being dogmatic. We may have differing views. 'Iron sharpens iron'. We can help one another.

- ✓ It's not about being reminded that you're a failure and being told to 'pull your socks up'!

- ✓ We're just ordinary blokes exploring matters of faith and spirituality.

- ✓ We're just ordinary blokes wanting some back-up.

- ✓ We will have some accountability. It's all too easy to live like the Lone Ranger, hiding behind some mask or other. I find it helpful to have a few blokes with whom I can share my struggles, my joy, my pain. I don't think that's a sign of weakness. I think it's a healthy thing to do.

- ✓ Our meetings are confidential. With accountability comes another important ingredient - confidentiality. By all means give others the general gist of what's gone on, but please don't pass on any personal information. Any personal stuff we share with one another stays in this room.

- ✓ Mentoring – as we have a mixed age group there is a sense of older guys helping younger men through the choppy waters of life, and of passing on wisdom for living. In return the younger men bring a freshness, energy and their own insights to the group.

However, it's not just about sitting around, trying to sort out our issues. Men prefer challenge and action rather than talking and abstract concepts. I need to find something purposeful to do and in the process some of my own issues get shunted out and diminish. Gathering men of faith together in a small group is a good place to start. Banter, yes. Have a laugh, yes. It's an essential part of friendship; but there is so much more!

Ready to go beyond the banter?

On the following pages you will find some more questions to get stuck into. They can be used by an individual reader for personal reflection or read out loud by the leader of a men's group to kick start a discussion.

WORK: Chapter one focuses on work, or indeed the lack of it. It opens up a conversation about where we get our identity from, the dangers of burn out, what success looks like, the tension between what's really written on our hearts and the need to pay the bills, and the importance of collaboration.

BANTER
What was the first job you ever had?
What's the worst job you've ever had?
Is there something you do which not many people know about?

BEYOND THE BANTER
If money wasn't a problem, what would you do with your life?
What skill or experience could you offer to others?
Can you collaborate with others to build something worthwhile?

STUFF: The quotation from Adi Alsaid is perhaps the key point when he says that technology provides so many different channels of loneliness. Technology can have some really useful applications but blokes need to guard against becoming isolated, self-contained and unaccountable.

BANTER
If money was no object what gadget would you buy?
What's the worst gadget you've ever owned?
Do you prefer sat-nav or a map? Have you ever been in a bit of a fog?

BEYOND THE BANTER
Have you ever felt lost spiritually?
Have you ever overstretched yourself financially?
Are you addicted to any gadget?

COMMUNITY: Following on from conversation about loneliness and isolation are some thoughts about our experience of community. Some activities we are involved in might promote cohesion, tolerance and understanding whilst others might tend to fragment a community. We may be in a community but not feel a sense of belonging.

BANTER
Have you ever had the experience of your neighbourhood being flooded?
Do you have a favourite charity?

BEYOND THE BANTER
What sort of things tend to fragment a community?
When was the last time you were part of something worthwhile?
How can you help other blokes to feel a sense of belonging to something?

MUSIC enables both individual and corporate expression. It can have a profound influence upon our mood. It's the accompaniment to both our celebrations and our sorrows. We may vary in our tastes but we can all identify pieces of music which speak to us in some way.

BANTER

What is your favourite piece of music and why?

What is your experience of a Jam Night or an Open Mic Night?

Do you have a longing to be a musician and if so what instrument would you play?

BEYOND THE BANTER

What part has music played in your spiritual journey?

What would life be like without music?

Has music inspired you to do something?

Have you been to a church where the sung worship was difficult to engage with or too performance orientated?

WAR AND PEACE: News of war or conflict is always in the headlines. For some there is a direct impact of loss of homes, livelihoods and loved ones. For others the impact is indirect raising fears and insecurities. This topic raises uncomfortable questions about the world we live in, and what our response is to those who have lost heart and seek refuge.

BANTER
What's the most impressive castle you've ever visited?
Has anyone you know been involved in a war?
How did you react when 9/11 happened?

BEYOND THE BANTER
Have you ever lost heart and sought refuge?
Have you ever lost friends, family, possessions or dignity?
Is there something which you did that resulted in conflict?
Do you feel that your story is important – that your life has meaning and purpose?

ADVENTURE: Boys identify with super heroes and in their play times act out some role or other where they try to save the world against impossible odds. Stories, myths and legends shape their thinking. As they grow into young men, relationships, careers and responsibilities might bury the sense of freedom they knew as a boy. Whilst some may pursue their dreams, others may look for adventure in unhelpful or self-destructive ways.

BANTER
Were your parents adventurous or did they play it safe?
When was the last time you went on an adventure?
How much of a risk taker are you?

BEYOND THE BANTER
Do you consider yourself to be a pioneer or a settler?
What injustice can you fight for?
What hope can you bring to desperate situations?
How can you release prisoners from darkness?

INFLUENCES: People and places can influence us either positively or negatively. Our parents and our home environment will initially have been an influence. Family, friends and the workplace may also have been significant. What we watch on television or see on film, what we read on line or in print will shape our views. Our experience of church will also mould our thinking, behaviours and beliefs.

BANTER
What can you remember about your childhood and hometown?
What kind of influence did your parents have on you?
Do you consider yourself to be tough or tender?

BEYOND THE BANTER
Who has been a great influence in your life?
In your experience of church has the thermostat been set in favour of feminine values such as love, feelings and sharing?
If you don't want to engage with others, what activities do you hide in?
Do you feel that you are making a difference in the lives of others?

SEASONS: Christmas and New Year are times when some are fortunate enough to have a break from work. It's a welcome pause in the middle of winter. But while some look forward to Christmas, many are uncomfortable with consumerism. Men of faith in particular can express concerns that the reason for the celebration is becoming buried under tinsel and wrapping paper.

BANTER
What's your favourite Christmas song?
What the best thing about Christmas?
What aspects of Christmas do you not enjoy?
What do you think about fireworks?

BEYOND THE BANTER
What memories does Christmas awaken?
How do you feel about seeing relatives over Christmas?
How significant is the Christmas story for you?

FAITH: For some blokes faith is a bolt-on optional extra to everyday life. Beliefs don't affect much of the way they think or behave. For others faith is the alpha and omega infiltrating every area of their lives. Expressions of faith vary enormously across the world and might include highly ritualistic and liturgical gatherings, simple meals around a table and quick fire prayers in an emergency. For some faith is evident through helping those in need. For others it's more about a personal encounter with God.

BANTER
What stuff do you keep in your attic?
What things in life do you find soul destroying?
What's the most epic thing you've ever done?

BEYOND THE BANTER
On a scale of one to ten how strong is your faith right now?
Do you feel like you're running on empty?
Do you have a strange fascination with the darkness?
Is there more to church than just a place of refuge?

HOPE: Worry is rife and suicide is the number one killer in the UK, in men under the age of forty. Dreadful things happen in our world and there's no satisfactory reason why. We may need to let go of our expectations for a trouble-free life and accept that joy and pain run side by side. So how can we become more hopeful ourselves and how can we help others who are struggling?

BANTER
Do you know anyone who blagged their way into a position of responsibility?
What sort of things do you get anxious about?
What is it about getting away from it all that you enjoy?

BEYOND THE BANTER
Can you identify with the idea of silent acceptance?
In a difficult situation do you feel the need to prove that you have what it takes?
Would you define hope as just a vague optimism?
How do you feel towards those who seem without hope?

Level Zero

Christian Vision for Men (CVM) currently have a four level strategy for connecting with un-churched blokes. Check out their website for more details but in brief: Level One is about blessing your friends by creating non-churchy events where non-churchy blokes can simply feel included in the banter. Level two is about blessing your friends by creating social events with a guest speaker who may raise matters which go beyond the banter. Level three is about blessing your friends (if they're interested) with an exploration of faith where questions can be answered in more depth. Level four is bloke friendly church, where men are encouraged to be all that God is calling them to be.

As I've gathered men of faith I've experienced three shocking realisations.

Firstly: We don't talk to each other. Ok, there's some banter, sometimes. But we don't share anything vital, there's no exchange of meaningful information, we don't discuss our views, our struggles, our defeats or celebrate our victories. I mean not at all, there's a kind of lock down, a no go area, a so far and not any further mentality.

Time and time again following our fairly open discussion groups a surprised individual tells me: "I've been coming to church for X number of years and I've never talked about any of this stuff" or "this is so different from my weekly bible study, I never knew what anyone else thought about X, Y, or Z before, this discussion has helped shape my thinking."

Secondly: We hardly know each other. Not properly. Again after our meetings so many men say something along the lines of: "I thought so-and-so had it all together, I didn't know he struggled with depression" or "I always thought so-and-so was a stuffed shirt, but now I've seen another side to him and he's actually an ok guy."

Thirdly: Partly because of the first two factors there is not as much depth to our unity as there might be. These are good, faithful men who are not actively dis-united. And yes, there are little pockets of unity here and there. But I think it's fair to say we are more like a collection of individuals than a driving force working together on some great mission.

The way I see it, there is great value in building a foundation of friendship and unity among men of faith, ahead of the game, off the pitch, as it were. I call this foundational stage of the journey Level Zero. That said, part of our meeting might also be defined as church for men, what CVM terms Level Four.

We are blessed with an abundance of theologians and therapists in the church. Good folk who are willing, trained and equipped to tackle the deepest issues of life. I am not an expert in therapy or theology, my calling is simply to help men quench their thirst for brotherhood.

Bob Fraser
bob.fraser@cvm.org.uk

RESOURCES FOR FURTHER THINKING

There is currently a wealth of material relating to Men's Ministry, and what some might refer to, as the emerging 'men's movement'. It's my hope that you (just as I have) will prayerfully consider some of the following works with an open mind. Weigh their arguments carefully. Chew over the points they raise. Balance them against your own experience. Don't be afraid to question or challenge some of the new thinking outlined here, or indeed old thinking. We're thinking creatures. We have the ability to understand, reason, figure things out and take ownership of concepts for ourselves. I believe it's ok to shift our position a little, or at least to view it from a fresh perspective.

Although the views are constantly changing and opening up while ascending a mountain the mountain remains the same. But our understanding of it shifts with each step taken. This process can actually be quite unsettling. When tackled alone it's all too easy to lose your bearings. Familiar landmarks appear differently and we head back to low ground in fear of the unknown. But just like hill walking, when a conversation about life and faith is worked out alongside trusted friends, the shared discoveries are all the more memorable.

Books worth reading

Epic by John Eldredge
Thomas Nelson Publishers 2004

Wild at Heart by John Eldredge
Thomas Nelson Publishers 2001

Why Men Hate Going to Church by David Murrow
Nelson Books 2005

The Blokes Bible by Dave Hopwood
Authentic Media 2006

Thank God it's Monday by Mark Greene
Scripture Union 2005

I am not my Father by Paul Scanlon
Abundant Life Publishing 2007

Fathered by God by John Eldredge
Thomas Nelson 2009

Second Choice by Viv Thomas
Paternoster Press 2000

The Map by David Murrow
Thomas Nelson 2010

The Prodigal God by Timothy Keller
Hodder and Stoughton 2009

We Make the Road by Walking by Brian McLaren
Hodder and Stoughton 2014

Manhood by Steve Biddulph
Finch Publishing, Sydney 2002

The Message by Eugene Peterson
Navpress, Colorado 2002

Where is God When it Hurts by Phillip Yancey
Zondervan 1990

Every Man's Battle by Stephen Arterburn and Fred Stoeker
Waterbrook Press 2013

Managing Your Time by Steve Chalke
Kingsway Publications 1998

The Return of the Prodigal Son by Henri JM Nouwen
Darton, Longman and Todd 1994

Love Wins by Rob Bell
Collins 2012

Father Fiction by Donald Miller
Hodder and Stoughton 2010

Cut to the Chase by Lee Jackson, Baz Gascoyne and Friends
Authentic Media 2006

Men Behaving Boldly by Paul Wallace
Triangle Books 1995

Tender Warrior by Stu
Weber Scripture Press 1995

Diamond Geezers by Anthony Delaney
River Publishing and Media 2011

The Daily Male by Nick Battle
Authentic Media 2008

Waking the Dead by John Eldredge
Thomas Nelson 2003

No More Heroes by Dave Hopwood
Authentic Media 2009

Christian Vision for Men (CVM) is a British organization who do a great job of producing excellent resources for men and men's groups, including books, film and audio. They run local meetings, national conferences and training events. CVM have a clear understanding of the real issues facing men both inside and outside of the church. It's well worth looking at the many resources on their website www.cvm.org.

Books for small group discussions include The Code, The Manual and Man Prayer all by Carl Beech

Videos: CVM have videos on Vimeo and YouTube Listen to CVM podcasts at www.cvm.org/podcasts. They include Shed Talk, produced by CVM for Premier Christian Radio, Team CVM and Men's Days.

Paul Scanlon is a world class, inspirational speaker. He is the former pastor of Abundant Life Church, Bradford. I've had the privilege of hearing him speak many times at XCEL, their annual conference for men. He has a relevant approach, and communicates crystal clear thinking. No wonder he's gone on to become a speaker around the globe on leadership, communication and building people. As a man from the north of England myself, I love Scanlon's warm northern tones, funny anecdotes and calm, clear delivery. I can listen to this guy for hours (especially while driving) and I bought most of the titles below as audio CDs. Many are still available via his web site - www.paulscanlon.com/store

Change
Events Versus Process
Jesus the Light of the World
We are Male by Birth but Men by Choice
Vital Friends
The Ugly Duckling
The Power of a Positive No
Strategic Quitting
From Relevant to Relic
Failure is not Terminal
The Thinking Heart
Destiny
Principles of Healthy Living
Raised but not Released
The Power of Inclusion
Prospering in the Prime of Life
Be a Self Feeder
Ageing Well
The Tyranny of Things
No More Sour Grapes
No More Christian Nice Guy
Others

Sorted Magazine is a top quality, British, bi-monthly, glossy magazine for men of faith. It's huge –122 pages! Big name Christian writers cover relevant topics which include culture, sport, cars, sex, fitness, tech, humour, lifestyle, advice and comment. Also available on-line: www.sortedmag.com

DISCLAIMER

Individual readers and Group Leaders are advised that this book, **Beyond the Banter**, is primarily a resource for men who would identify themselves with the Christian faith and who want to connect with others in a small group setting. Hence the author has not referenced any overtly evangelical resources.

Individual readers and Group Leaders are advised that this book, **Beyond the Banter**, along with the practise of meeting together in a men's group, are in no way substitutes for professional counselling and/or medical help.

The complexities of mental health are way beyond the scope of the untrained. Therefore Group Leaders should take great care to direct members towards seeking professional help if they are at all worried. Individual readers should speak to their doctor if they are concerned about their own mental wellbeing.

The views expressed in **Beyond the Banter** are the author's own and names have been changed to preserve confidentiality.

Biography in brief

Bob Fraser has a background in the predominantly male environment of professional building design, construction and project management. Bob also trained as a teacher. He is perhaps better known by many as a prolific singer songwriter, performing and leading music teams and bands in prisons, schools, colleges, universities, folk clubs, pubs and churches. He was one of the early pioneers of contemporary Christian music in the UK, recording two vinyl albums as front man with the popular 70s country rock band Canaan, and playing with them at prestigious venues including The Royal Albert Hall in London and the Usher Hall in Edinburgh. Bob has twelve solo albums and a further ten include his songs and vocals. His most recent album includes songs which were commissioned to mark the centenary of the Great War.

Bob runs a group for men of faith which has grown to capacity. The group provides a safe place to belong, express views about life and faith and build friendship. Bob currently works in restorative justice with male offenders in prison. He is also CVM Regional Director England (North West).

In 2006 Bob began to work through some thinking about masculinity and faith in God. With too many thoughts to squeeze into a song he turned his hand to writing longer articles and blogs. These pieces eventually grew and developed into a full blown manuscript and his first book, **Beyond the Banter**, was published.

About inhousemedia

Inhousemedia is an emerging, independent micro-publisher based in the North West of England. Operationally we function as a non-profit, project-based co-operative. We specialize in creating original resources which are locally and lovingly produced, sympathetic to the Christian faith and mindful of ethical values.

Our products are available to buy online and at live events. Prices are kept as low as possible - all CDs are a fiver . We regularly raise funds for our favourite charities.

While our books and music CDs have faith elements within them, and are underpinned by a faith in God, we hope they are gentle enough to be valued and enjoyed by those on the fringes of faith communities and beyond.

RESOURCES FROM
Inhousemedia

Life in Cardigans is a great gift for the woman in your life! She will love this rich collection of stories each inspired by at least one cardigan. From the beautiful hand-knitted creation gifted from a special auntie to the mass produced synthetic rag worn only for painting and cleaning, these touching and often funny stories, discover worth and meaning in something as ordinary as a cardigan. Available as a paperback or e-book from Amazon and all good online bookstores. Get the latest news from Inhousemedia and connect with Val on Twitter @ValFraserAuthor.

RESOURCES FROM

inhousemedia

The latest Bob Fraser audio CDs are packed with original songs and are available in both hard copy format and as digital downloads. Have a quick listen and buy at www.bob.frasermusic.com

www.ingramcontent.com/pod-product-compliance
Lightning Source LLC
Chambersburg PA
CBHW050538300426
44113CB00012B/2163